Cyber Attacks

"Dr. Amoroso's fifth book *Cyber Attacks: Protecting National Infrastructure* outlines the challenges of protecting our nation's infrastructure from cyber attack using security techniques established to protect much smaller and less complex environments. He proposes a brand new type of national infrastructure protection methodology and outlines a strategy presented as a series of ten basic design and operations principles ranging from deception to response. The bulk of the text covers each of these principles in technical detail. While several of these principles would be daunting to implement and practice they provide the first clear and concise framework for discussion of this critical challenge. This text is thought-provoking and should be a 'must read' for anyone concerned with cybersecurity in the private or government sector."

—**Clayton W. Naeve, Ph.D.**,
Senior Vice President and Chief Information Officer,
Endowed Chair in Bioinformatics,
St. Jude Children's Research Hospital,
Memphis, TN

"Dr. Ed Amoroso reveals in plain English the threats and weaknesses of our critical infrastructure balanced against practices that reduce the exposures. This is an excellent guide to the understanding of the cyber-scape that the security professional navigates. The book takes complex concepts of security and simplifies it into coherent and simple to understand concepts."

—**Arnold Felberbaum**,
Chief IT Security & Compliance Officer,
Reed Elsevier

"The national infrastructure, which is now vital to communication, commerce and entertainment in everyday life, is highly vulnerable to malicious attacks and terrorist threats. Today, it is possible for botnets to penetrate millions of computers around the world in few minutes, and to attack the valuable national infrastructure.

"As the *New York Times* reported, the growing number of threats by botnets suggests that this cyber security issue has become a serious problem, and we are losing the war against these attacks.

"While computer security technologies will be useful for network systems, the reality tells us that this conventional approach is not effective enough for the complex, large-scale national infrastructure.

"Not only does the author provide comprehensive methodologies based on 25 years of experience in cyber security at AT&T, but he also suggests 'security through obscurity,' which attempts to use secrecy to provide security."

—**Byeong Gi Lee**,
President, IEEE Communications Society, and
Commissioner of the Korea Communications Commission (KCC)

Cyber Attacks
Protecting National Infrastructure

Edward G. Amoroso

AMSTERDAM • BOSTON • HEIDELBERG • LONDON
NEW YORK • OXFORD • PARIS • SAN DIEGO
SAN FRANCISCO • SINGAPORE • SYDNEY • TOKYO
Butterworth-Heinemann is an imprint of Elsevier

Acquiring Editor: Pam Chester
Development Editor: Gregory Chalson
Project Manager: Paul Gottehrer
Designer: Alisa Andreola

Butterworth-Heinemann is an imprint of Elsevier
30 Corporate Drive, Suite 400, Burlington, MA 01803, USA

Library of Congress Cataloging-in-Publication Data
Amoroso, Edward G.
  Cyber attacks : protecting national infrastructure / Edward Amoroso.
    p. cm.
  Includes index.
  ISBN 978-0-12-384917-5
  1. Cyberterrorism—United States—Prevention. 2. Computer security—United States. 3. National security—United States. I. Title.
  HV6773.2.A47 2011
  363.325′90046780973—dc22   2010040626

British Library Cataloguing-in-Publication Data
A catalogue record for this book is available from the British Library.

Printed in the United States of America
10 11 12 13 14   10 9 8 7 6 5 4 3 2 1

For information on all BH publications visit our website at www.elsevierdirect.com/security

HV
6773.2
A47
2011

CONTENTS

PREFACE

Man did not enter into society to become worse than he was before, nor to have fewer rights than he had before, but to have those rights better secured.

Thomas Paine in *Common Sense*

Before you invest any of your time with this book, please take a moment and look over the following points. They outline my basic philosophy of national infrastructure security. I think that your reaction to these points will give you a pretty good idea of what your reaction will be to the book.

1. Citizens of free nations cannot hope to express or enjoy their freedoms if basic security protections are not provided. Security does not suppress freedom—it makes freedom possible.
2. In virtually every modern nation, computers and networks power critical infrastructure elements. As a result, cyber attackers can use computers and networks to damage or ruin the infrastructures that citizens rely on.
3. Security protections, such as those in security books, were designed for small-scale environments such as enterprise computing environments. These protections do not extrapolate to the protection of massively complex infrastructure.
4. Effective national cyber protections will be driven largely by cooperation and coordination between commercial, industrial, and government organizations. Thus, organizational management issues will be as important to national defense as technical issues.
5. Security is a process of risk reduction, not risk removal. Therefore, concrete steps can and should be taken to reduce, but not remove, the risk of cyber attack to national infrastructure.
6. The current risk of catastrophic cyber attack to national infrastructure must be viewed as extremely high, by any realistic measure. Taking little or no action to reduce this risk would be a foolish national decision.

The chapters of this book are organized around ten basic principles that *will* reduce the risk of cyber attack to national infrastructure in a substantive manner. They are driven by experiences gained managing the security of one of the largest, most complex infrastructures in the world, by years of learning from various commercial and government organizations, and by years of interaction with students and academic researchers in the security field. They are also driven by personal experiences dealing with a wide range of successful and unsuccessful cyber attacks, including ones directed at infrastructure of considerable value. The implementation of the ten principles in this book will require national resolve and changes to the way computing and networking elements are designed, built, and operated in the context of national infrastructure. My hope is that the suggestions offered in these pages will make this process easier.

ACKNOWLEDGMENT

The cyber security experts in the AT&T Chief Security Office, my colleagues across AT&T Labs and the AT&T Chief Technology Office, my colleagues across the entire AT&T business, and my graduate and undergraduate students in the Computer Science Department at the Stevens Institute of Technology, have had a profound impact on my thinking and on the contents of this book. In addition, many prominent enterprise customers of AT&T with whom I've had the pleasure of serving, especially those in the United States Federal Government, have been great influencers in the preparation of this material.

I'd also like to extend a great thanks to my wife Lee, daughter Stephanie (17), son Matthew (15), and daughter Alicia (9) for their collective patience with my busy schedule.

Edward G. Amoroso
Florham Park, NJ
September 2010

INTRODUCTION

Somewhere in his writings—and I regret having forgotten where—
John Von Neumann draws attention to what seemed to him a
contrast. He remarked that for simple mechanisms it is often
easier to describe how they work than what they do, while for more
complicated mechanisms it was usually the other way round.

Edsger W. Dijkstra[1]

National infrastructure refers to the complex, underlying delivery
and support systems for all large-scale services considered absolutely essential to a nation. These services include emergency
response, law enforcement databases, supervisory control and
data acquisition (SCADA) systems, power control networks, military support services, consumer entertainment systems, financial
applications, and mobile telecommunications. Some national
services are provided directly by government, but most are provided by commercial groups such as Internet service providers, airlines, and banks. In addition, certain services considered
essential to one nation might include infrastructure support that
is controlled by organizations from another nation. This global
interdependency is consistent with the trends referred to collectively by Thomas Friedman as a "flat world."[2]

National infrastructure, especially in the United States, has
always been vulnerable to malicious physical attacks such as
equipment tampering, cable cuts, facility bombing, and asset
theft. The events of September 11, 2001, for example, are the
most prominent and recent instance of a massive physical attack
directed at national infrastructure. During the past couple of
decades, however, vast portions of national infrastructure have
become reliant on software, computers, and networks. This reliance typically includes remote access, often over the Internet, to

---

[1] E.W. Dijkstra, *Selected Writings on Computing: A Personal Perspective*, Springer-Verlag,
New York, 1982, pp. 212–213.
[2] T. Friedman, *The World Is Flat: A Brief History of the Twenty-First Century*, Farrar,
Straus, and Giroux, New York, 2007. (Friedman provides a useful economic backdrop to
the global aspect of the cyber attack trends suggested in this chapter.)

Cyber Attacks. DOI: 10.1016/B978-0-12-384917-5.00001-9

1

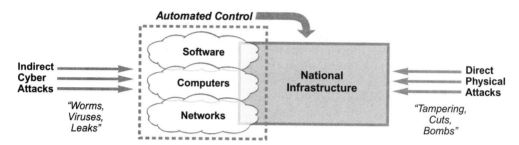

Figure 1.1 National infrastructure cyber and physical attacks.

the systems that control national services. Adversaries thus can initiate cyber attacks on infrastructure using worms, viruses, leaks, and the like. These attacks indirectly target national infrastructure through their associated automated controls systems (see Figure 1.1).

A seemingly obvious approach to dealing with this national cyber threat would involve the use of well-known computer security techniques. After all, computer security has matured substantially in the past couple of decades, and considerable expertise now exists on how to protect software, computers, and networks. In such a national scheme, safeguards such as firewalls, intrusion detection systems, antivirus software, passwords, scanners, audit trails, and encryption would be directly embedded into infrastructure, just as they are currently in small-scale environments. These national security systems would be connected to a centralized threat management system, and incident response would follow a familiar sort of enterprise process. Furthermore, to ensure security policy compliance, one would expect the usual programs of end-user awareness, security training, and third-party audit to be directed toward the people building and operating national infrastructure. Virtually every national infrastructure protection initiative proposed to date has followed this seemingly straightforward path.[3]

While well-known computer security techniques will certainly be useful for national infrastructure, most practical experience to date suggests that this conventional approach will not be sufficient. A primary reason is the size, scale, and scope inherent in complex national infrastructure. For example, where an enterprise might involve manageably sized assets, national infrastructure will require unusually powerful computing support with the ability to handle enormous volumes of data. Such volumes

[3] Executive Office of the President, *Cyberspace Policy Review: Assuring a Trusted and Resilient Information and Communications Infrastructure*, U.S. White House, Washington, D.C., 2009 (http://handle.dtic.mil/100.2/ADA501541).

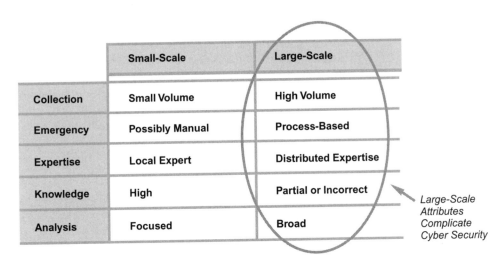

	Small-Scale	Large-Scale
Collection	Small Volume	High Volume
Emergency	Possibly Manual	Process-Based
Expertise	Local Expert	Distributed Expertise
Knowledge	High	Partial or Incorrect
Analysis	Focused	Broad

Large-Scale Attributes Complicate Cyber Security

Figure 1.2 Differences between small- and large-scale cyber security.

will easily exceed the storage and processing capacity of typical enterprise security tools such as a commercial threat management system. Unfortunately, this incompatibility conflicts with current initiatives in government and industry to reduce costs through the use of common commercial off-the-shelf products.

In addition, whereas enterprise systems can rely on manual intervention by a local expert during a security disaster, large-scale national infrastructure generally requires a carefully orchestrated response by teams of security experts using predetermined processes. These teams of experts will often work in different groups, organizations, or even countries. In the worst cases, they will cooperate only if forced by government, often sharing just the minimum amount of information to avoid legal consequences. An additional problem is that the complexity associated with national infrastructure leads to the bizarre situation where response teams often have partial or incorrect understanding about how the underlying systems work. For these reasons, seemingly convenient attempts to apply existing small-scale security processes to large-scale infrastructure attacks will ultimately fail (see Figure 1.2).

As a result, a brand-new type of national infrastructure protection methodology is required—one that combines the best elements of existing computer and network security techniques with the unique and difficult challenges associated with complex, large-scale national services. This book offers just such a protection methodology for national infrastructure. It is based on a quarter century of practical experience designing, building, and operating

National infrastructure databases far exceed the size of even the largest commercial databases.

cyber security systems for government, commercial, and consumer infrastructure. It is represented as a series of protection principles that can be applied to new or existing systems. Because of the unique needs of national infrastructure, especially its massive size, scale, and scope, some aspects of the methodology will be unfamiliar to the computer security community. In fact, certain elements of the approach, such as our favorable view of "security through obscurity," might appear in direct conflict with conventional views of how computers and networks should be protected.

National Cyber Threats, Vulnerabilities, and Attacks

Conventional computer security is based on the oft-repeated taxonomy of security threats which includes confidentiality, integrity, availability, and theft. In the broadest sense, all four diverse threat types will have applicability in national infrastructure. For example, protections are required equally to deal with sensitive information leaks (confidentiality), worms affecting the operation of some critical application (integrity), botnets knocking out an important system (availability), or citizens having their identities compromised (theft). Certainly, the availability threat to national services must be viewed as particularly important, given the nature of the threat and its relation to national assets. One should thus expect particular attention to availability threats to national infrastructure. Nevertheless, it makes sense to acknowledge that all four types of security threats in the conventional taxonomy of computer security must be addressed in any national infrastructure protection methodology.

Vulnerabilities are more difficult to associate with any taxonomy. Obviously, national infrastructure must address well-known problems such as improperly configured equipment, poorly designed local area networks, unpatched system software, exploitable bugs in application code, and locally disgruntled employees. The problem is that the most fundamental vulnerability in national infrastructure involves the staggering complexity inherent in the underlying systems. This complexity is so pervasive that many times security incidents uncover aspects of computing functionality that were previously unknown to anyone, including sometimes the system designers. Furthermore, in certain cases, the optimal security solution involves simplifying and cleaning up poorly conceived infrastructure. This is bad news, because most large organizations are inept at simplifying much of anything.

The best one can do for a comprehensive view of the vulnerabilities associated with national infrastructure is to address their

> Any of the most common security concerns—confidentiality, integrity, availability, and theft—threaten our national infrastructure.

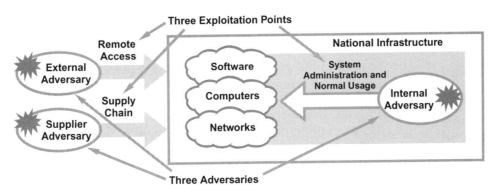

Figure 1.3 Adversaries and exploitation points in national infrastructure.

relative exploitation points. This can be done with an abstract national infrastructure cyber security model that includes three types of malicious adversaries: *external adversary* (hackers on the Internet), *internal adversary* (trusted insiders), and *supplier adversary* (vendors and partners). Using this model, three exploitation points emerge for national infrastructure: *remote access* (Internet and telework), *system administration and normal usage* (management and use of software, computers, and networks), and *supply chain* (procurement and outsourcing) (see Figure 1.3).

These three exploitation points and three types of adversaries can be associated with a variety of possible motivations for initiating either a full or test attack on national infrastructure.

Five Possible Motivations for an Infrastructure Attack

- *Country-sponsored warfare*—National infrastructure attacks sponsored and funded by enemy countries must be considered the most significant potential motivation, because the intensity of adversary capability and willingness to attack is potentially unlimited.
- *Terrorist attack*—The terrorist motivation is also significant, especially because groups driven by terror can easily obtain sufficient capability and funding to perform significant attacks on infrastructure.
- *Commercially motivated attack*—When one company chooses to utilize cyber attacks to gain a commercial advantage, it becomes a national infrastructure incident if the target company is a purveyor of some national asset.
- *Financially driven criminal attack*—Identify theft is the most common example of a financially driven attack by criminal groups, but other cases exist, such as companies being extorted to avoid a cyber incident.
- *Hacking*—One must not forget that many types of attacks are still driven by the motivation of hackers, who are often just mischievous youths trying to learn or to build a reputation within the hacking community. This is much less a sinister motivation, and national leaders should try to identify better ways to tap this boundless capability and energy.

Each of the three exploitation points might be utilized in a cyber attack on national infrastructure. For example, a supplier might use a poorly designed supply chain to insert Trojan horse code into a software component that controls some national asset, or a hacker on the Internet might take advantage of some unprotected Internet access point to break into a vulnerable service. Similarly, an insider might use trusted access for either system administration or normal system usage to create an attack. The potential also exists for an external adversary to gain valuable insider access through patient, measured means, such as gaining employment in an infrastructure-supporting organization and then becoming trusted through a long process of work performance. In each case, the possibility exists that a limited type of engagement might be performed as part of a planned test or exercise. This seems especially likely if the attack is country or terrorist sponsored, because it is consistent with past practice.

At each exploitation point, the vulnerability being used might be a well-known problem previously reported in an authoritative public advisory, or it could be a proprietary issue kept hidden by a local organization. It is entirely appropriate for a recognized authority to make a detailed public vulnerability advisory if the benefits of notifying the good guys outweigh the risks of alerting the bad guys. This cost–benefit result usually occurs when many organizations can directly benefit from the information and can thus take immediate action. When the reported vulnerability is unique and isolated, however, then reporting the details might be irresponsible, especially if the notification process does not enable a more timely fix. This is a key issue, because many government authorities continue to consider new rules for mandatory reporting. If the information being demanded is not properly protected, then the reporting process might result in more harm than good.

> When to issue a vulnerability risk advisory and when to keep the risk confidential must be determined on a case-by-case basis, depending on the threat.

Botnet Threat

Perhaps the most insidious type of attack that exists today is the *botnet*.[4] In short, a botnet involves remote control of a collection of compromised end-user machines, usually broadband-connected PCs. The controlled end-user machines, which are referred to as *bots*, are programmed to attack some target that is designated by the botnet controller. The attack is tough to stop

---

[4] Much of the material on botnets in this chapter is derived from work done by Brian Rexroad, David Gross, and several others from AT&T.

because end-user machines are typically administered in an ineffective manner. Furthermore, once the attack begins, it occurs from sources potentially scattered across geographic, political, and service provider boundaries. Perhaps worse, bots are programmed to take commands from multiple controller systems, so any attempts to destroy a given controller result in the bots simply homing to another one.

The Five Entities That Comprise a Botnet Attack

- *Botnet operator*—This is the individual, group, or country that creates the botnet, including its setup and operation. When the botnet is used for financial gain, it is the operator who will benefit. Law enforcement and cyber security initiatives have found it very difficult to identify the operators. The press, in particular, has done a poor job reporting on the presumed identity of botnet operators, often suggesting sponsorship by some country when little supporting evidence exists.
- *Botnet controller*—This is the set of servers that command and control the operation of a botnet. Usually these servers have been maliciously compromised for this purpose. Many times, the real owner of a server that has been compromised will not even realize what has occurred. The type of activity directed by a controller includes all recruitment, setup, communication, and attack activity. Typical botnets include a handful of controllers, usually distributed across the globe in a non-obvious manner.
- *Collection of bots*—These are the end-user, broadband-connected PCs infected with botnet malware. They are usually owned and operated by normal citizens, who become unwitting and unknowing dupes in a botnet attack. When a botnet includes a concentration of PCs in a given region, observers often incorrectly attribute the attack to that region. The use of smart mobile devices in a botnet will grow as upstream capacity and device processing power increase.
- *Botnet software drop*—Most botnets include servers designed to store software that might be useful for the botnets during their lifecycle. Military personnel might refer to this as an *arsenal*. Like controllers, botnet software drop points are usually servers compromised for this purpose, often unknown to the normal server operator.
- *Botnet target*—This is the location that is targeted in the attack. Usually, it is a website, but it can really be any device, system, or network that is visible to the bots. In most cases, botnets target prominent and often controversial websites, simply because they are visible via the Internet and generally have a great deal at stake in terms of their availability. This increases gain and leverage for the attacker. Logically, however, botnets can target anything visible.

The way a botnet works is that the controller is set up to communicate with the bots via some designated protocol, most often Internet Relay Chat (IRC). This is done via malware inserted into the end-user PCs that comprise the bots. A great challenge in this regard is that home PCs and laptops are so poorly administered. Amazingly, over time, the day-to-day system and security administration task for home computers has gravitated to the end user.

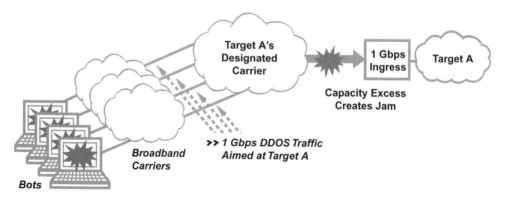

Figure 1.4 Sample DDOS attack from a botnet.

This obligation results in both a poor user experience and general dissatisfaction with the security task. For example, when a typical computer buyer brings a new machine home, it has probably been preloaded with security software by the retailer. From this point onward, however, that home buyer is then tasked with all responsibility for protecting the machine. This includes keeping firewall, intrusion detection, antivirus, and antispam software up to date, as well as ensuring that all software patches are current. When these tasks are not well attended, the result is a more vulnerable machine that is easily turned into a bot. (Sadly, even if a machine is properly managed, expert bot software designers might find a way to install the malware anyway.)

Once a group of PCs has been compromised into bots, attacks can thus be launched by the controller via a command to the bots, which would then do as they are instructed. This might not occur instantaneously with the infection; in fact, experience suggests that many botnets lay dormant for a great deal of time. Nevertheless, all sorts of attacks are possible in a botnet arrangement, including the now-familiar *distributed denial of service attack* (DDOS). In such a case, the bots create more inbound traffic than the target gateway can handle. For example, if some theoretical gateway allows for 1 Gbps of inbound traffic, and the botnet creates an inbound stream larger than 1 Gbps, then a logjam results at the inbound gateway, and a denial of service condition occurs (see Figure 1.4).

Any serious present study of cyber security must acknowledge the unique threat posed by botnets. Virtually any Internet-connected system is vulnerable to major outages from a botnet-originated DDOS attack. The physics of the situation are especially depressing; that is, a botnet that might steal 500 Kbps

> Home PC users may never know they are being used for a botnet scheme.

> A DDOS attack is like a cyber traffic jam.

of upstream capacity from each bot (which would generally allow for concurrent normal computing and networking) would only need three bots to collapse a target T1 connection. Following this logic, only 16,000 bots would be required theoretically to fill up a 10-Gbps connection. Because most of the thousands of botnets that have been observed on the Internet are at least this size, the threat is obvious; however, many recent and prominent botnets such as Storm and Conficker are much larger, comprising as many as several million bots, so the threat to national infrastructure is severe and immediate.

National Cyber Security Methodology Components

Our proposed methodology for protecting national infrastructure is presented as a series of ten basic design and operation principles. The implication is that, by using these principles as a guide for either improving existing infrastructure components or building new ones, the security result will be desirable, including a reduced risk from botnets. The methodology addresses all four types of security threats to national infrastructure; it also deals with all three types of adversaries to national infrastructure, as well as the three exploitation points detailed in the infrastructure model. The list of principles in the methodology serves as a guide to the remainder of this chapter, as well as an outline for the remaining chapters of the book:

- *Chapter 2: Deception*—The openly advertised use of deception creates uncertainty for adversaries because they will not know if a discovered problem is real or a trap. The more common hidden use of deception allows for real-time behavioral analysis if an intruder is caught in a trap. Programs of national infrastructure protection must include the appropriate use of deception, especially to reduce the malicious partner and supplier risk.
- *Chapter 3: Separation*—Network separation is currently accomplished using firewalls, but programs of national infrastructure protection will require three specific changes. Specifically, national infrastructure must include network-based firewalls on high-capacity backbones to throttle DDOS attacks, internal firewalls to segregate infrastructure and reduce the risk of sabotage, and better tailoring of firewall features for specific applications such as SCADA protocols.[5]

---

[5] R. Kurtz, *Securing SCADA Systems*, Wiley, New York, 2006. (Kurtz provides an excellent overview of SCADA systems and the current state of the practice in securing them.)

- *Chapter 4: Diversity*—Maintaining diversity in the products, services, and technologies supporting national infrastructure reduces the chances that one common weakness can be exploited to produce a cascading attack. A massive program of coordinated procurement and supplier management is required to achieve a desired level of national diversity across all assets. This will be tough, because it conflicts with most cost-motivated information technology procurement initiatives designed to minimize diversity in infrastructure.
- *Chapter 5: Commonality*—The consistent use of security best practices in the administration of national infrastructure ensures that no infrastructure component is either poorly managed or left completely unguarded. National programs of standards selection and audit validation, especially with an emphasis on uniform programs of simplification, are thus required. This can certainly include citizen end users, but one should never rely on high levels of security compliance in the broad population.
- *Chapter 6: Depth*—The use of defense in depth in national infrastructure ensures that no critical asset is reliant on a single security layer; thus, if any layer should fail, an additional layer is always present to mitigate an attack. Analysis is required at the national level to ensure that all critical assets are protected by at least two layers, preferably more.
- *Chapter 7: Discretion*—The use of personal discretion in the sharing of information about national assets is a practical technique that many computer security experts find difficult to accept because it conflicts with popular views on "security through obscurity." Nevertheless, large-scale infrastructure protection cannot be done properly unless a national culture of discretion and secrecy is nurtured. It goes without saying that such discretion should never be put in place to obscure illegal or unethical practices.
- *Chapter 8: Collection*—The collection of audit log information is a necessary component of an infrastructure security scheme, but it introduces privacy, size, and scale issues not seen in smaller computer and network settings. National infrastructure protection will require a data collection approach that is acceptable to the citizenry and provides the requisite level of detail for security analysis.
- *Chapter 9: Correlation*—Correlation is the most fundamental of all analysis techniques for cyber security, but modern attack methods such as botnets greatly complicate its use for attack-related indicators. National-level correlation must be performed using all available sources and the best available

technology and algorithms. Correlating information around a botnet attack is one of the more challenging present tasks in cyber security.

- *Chapter 10: Awareness*—Maintaining situational awareness is more important in large-scale infrastructure protection than in traditional computer and network security because it helps to coordinate the real-time aspect of multiple infrastructure components. A program of national situational awareness must be in place to ensure proper management decision-making for national assets.
- *Chapter 11: Response*—Incident response for national infrastructure protection is especially difficult because it generally involves complex dependencies and interactions between disparate government and commercial groups. It is best accomplished at the national level when it focuses on early indications, rather than on incidents that have already begun to damage national assets.

The balance of this chapter will introduce each principle, with discussion on its current use in computer and network security, as well as its expected benefits for national infrastructure protection.

Deception

The principle of *deception* involves the deliberate introduction of misleading functionality or misinformation into national infrastructure for the purpose of tricking an adversary. The idea is that an adversary would be presented with a view of national infrastructure functionality that might include services or interface components that are present for the sole purpose of fakery. Computer scientists refer to this functionality as a *honey pot*, but the use of deception for national infrastructure could go far beyond this conventional view. Specifically, deception can be used to protect against certain types of cyber attacks that no other security method will handle. Law enforcement agencies have been using deception effectively for many years, often catching cyber stalkers and criminals by spoofing the reported identity of an end point. Even in the presence of such obvious success, however, the cyber security community has yet to embrace deception as a mainstream protection measure.

> Deception is an oft-used tool by law enforcement agencies to catch cyber stalkers and predators.

Deception in computing typically involves a layer of cleverly designed trap functionality strategically embedded into the internal and external interfaces for services. Stated more simply, deception involves fake functionality embedded into real interfaces. An example might be a deliberately planted trap link on

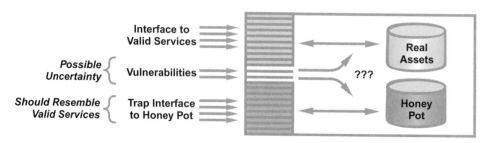

Figure 1.5 Components of an interface with deception.

a website that would lead potential intruders into an environment designed to highlight adversary behavior. When the deception is open and not secret, it might introduce uncertainty for adversaries in the exploitation of real vulnerabilities, because the adversary might suspect that the discovered entry point is a trap. When it is hidden and stealth, which is the more common situation, it serves as the basis for real-time forensic analysis of adversary behavior. In either case, the result is a public interface that includes real services, deliberate honey pot traps, and the inevitable exploitable vulnerabilities that unfortunately will be present in all nontrivial interfaces (see Figure 1.5).

Only relatively minor tests of honey pot technology have been reported to date, usually in the context of a research effort. Almost no reports are available on the day-to-day use of deception as a structural component of a real enterprise security program. In fact, the vast majority of security programs for companies, government agencies, and national infrastructure would include no such functionality. Academic computer scientists have shown little interest in this type of security, as evidenced by the relatively thin body of literature on the subject. This lack of interest might stem from the discomfort associated with using computing to mislead. Another explanation might be the relative ineffectiveness of deception against the botnet threat, which is clearly the most important security issue on the Internet today. Regardless of the cause, this tendency to avoid the use of deception is unfortunate, because many cyber attacks, such as subtle break-ins by trusted insiders and Trojan horses being maliciously inserted by suppliers into delivered software, cannot be easily remedied by any other means.

> Deception is less effective against botnets than other types of attack methods.

The most direct benefit of deception is that it enables forensic analysis of intruder activity. By using a honey pot, unique insights into attack methods can be gained by watching what is occurring in real time. Such deception obviously works best in a hidden, stealth mode, unknown to the intruder, because if the intruder realizes that some vulnerable exploitation point is a fake, then no exploitation will occur. Honey pot pioneers Cliff Stoll, Bill Cheswick, and Lance Spitzner have provided a majority of the reported experience in real-time forensics using honey pots. They have all suggested that the most difficult task involves creating believability in the trap. It is worth noting that connecting a honey pot to real assets is a terrible idea.

Do not connect honey pots to real assets!

An additional potential benefit of deception is that it can introduce the clever idea that some discovered vulnerability might instead be a deliberately placed trap. Obviously, such an approach is only effective if the use of deception is not hidden; that is, the adversary must know that deception is an approved and accepted technique used for protection. It should therefore be obvious that the major advantage here is that an accidental vulnerability, one that might previously have been an open door for an intruder, will suddenly look like a possible trap. A further profound notion, perhaps for open discussion, is whether just the *implied statement* that deception might be present (perhaps without real justification) would actually reduce risk. Suppliers, for example, might be less willing to take the risk of Trojan horse insertion if the procuring organization advertises an open research and development program of detailed software test and inspection against this type of attack.

Separation

The principle of *separation* involves enforcement of access policy restrictions on the users and resources in a computing environment. Access policy restrictions result in separation domains, which are arguably the most common security architectural concept in use today. This is good news, because the creation of access-policy-based separation domains will be essential in the protection of national infrastructure. Most companies today will typically use firewalls to create perimeters around their presumed enterprise, and access decisions are embedded in the associated rules sets. This use of enterprise firewalls for separation is complemented by several other common access techniques:

- *Authentication and identity management*—These methods are used to validate and manage the identities on which separation decisions are made. They are essential in every enterprise but cannot be relied upon solely for infrastructure security. Malicious insiders, for example, will be authorized under such systems. In addition, external attacks such as DDOS are unaffected by authentication and identity management.

- *Logical access controls*—The access controls inherent in operating systems and applications provide some degree of separation, but they are also weak in the presence of compromised insiders. Furthermore, underlying vulnerabilities in applications and operating systems can often be used to subvert these methods.
- *LAN controls*—Access control lists on local area network (LAN) components can provide separation based on information such as Internet Protocol (IP) or media access control (MAC) address. In this regard, they are very much like firewalls but typically do not extend their scope beyond an isolated segment.
- *Firewalls*—For large-scale infrastructure, firewalls are particularly useful, because they separate one network from another. Today, every Internet-based connection is almost certainly protected by some sort of firewall functionality. This approach worked especially well in the early years of the Internet, when the number of Internet connections to the enterprise was small. Firewalls do remain useful, however, even with the massive connectivity of most groups to the Internet. As a result, national infrastructure should continue to include the use of firewalls to protect known perimeter gateways to the Internet.

Given the massive scale and complexity associated with national infrastructure, three specific separation enhancements are required, and all are extensions of the firewall concept.

Required Separation Enhancements for National Infrastructure Protection

1. The use of network-based firewalls is absolutely required for many national infrastructure applications, especially ones vulnerable to DDOS attacks from the Internet. This use of network-based mediation can take advantage of high-capacity network backbones if the service provider is involved in running the firewalls.
2. The use of firewalls to segregate and isolate internal infrastructure components from one another is a mandatory technique for simplifying the implementation of access control policies in an organization. When insiders have malicious intent, any exploit they might attempt should be explicitly contained by internal firewalls.
3. The use of commercial off-the-shelf firewalls, especially for SCADA usage, will require tailoring of the firewall to the unique protocol needs of the application. It is not acceptable for national infrastructure protection to retrofit the use of a generic, commercial, off-the-shelf tool that is not optimized for its specific use (see Figure 1.6).

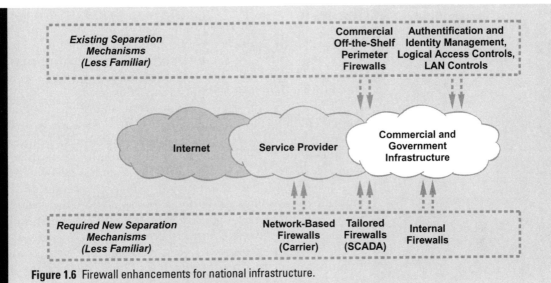

Figure 1.6 Firewall enhancements for national infrastructure.

With the advent of cloud computing, many enterprise and government agency security managers have come to acknowledge the benefits of network-based firewall processing. The approach scales well and helps to deal with the uncontrolled complexity one typically finds in national infrastructure. That said, the reality is that most national assets are still secured by placing a firewall at each of the hundreds or thousands of presumed choke points. This approach does not scale and leads to a false sense of security. It should also be recognized that the firewall is not the only device subjected to such scale problems. Intrusion detection systems, antivirus filtering, threat management, and denial of service filtering also require a network-based approach to function properly in national infrastructure.

An additional problem that exists in current national infrastructure is the relative lack of architectural separation used in an internal, trusted network. Most security engineers know that large systems are best protected by dividing them into smaller systems. Firewalls or packet filtering routers can be used to segregate an enterprise network into manageable domains. Unfortunately, the current state of the practice in infrastructure protection rarely includes a disciplined approach to separating internal assets. This is unfortunate, because it allows an intruder in one domain to have access to a more expansive view of the organizational infrastructure. The threat increases when the firewall has not been optimized for applications such as SCADA that require specialized protocol support.

Parceling a network into manageable smaller domains creates an environment that is easier to protect.

Diversity

The principle of *diversity* involves the selection and use of technology and systems that are intentionally different in substantive ways. These differences can include technology source, programming language, computing platform, physical location, and product vendor. For national infrastructure, realizing such diversity requires a coordinated program of procurement to ensure a proper mix of technologies and vendors. The purpose of introducing these differences is to deliberately create a measure of non-interoperability so that an attack cannot easily cascade from one component to another through exploitation of some common vulnerability. Certainly, it would be possible, even in a diverse environment, for an exploit to cascade, but the likelihood is reduced as the diversity profile increases.

This concept is somewhat controversial, because so much of computer science theory and information technology practice in the past couple of decades has been focused on maximizing interoperability of technologies. This might help explain the relative lack of attentiveness that diversity considerations receive in these fields. By way of analogy, however, cyber attacks on national infrastructure are mitigated by diversity technology just as disease propagation is reduced by a diverse biological ecosystem. That is, a problem that originates in one area of infrastructure with the intention of automatic propagation will only succeed in the presence of some degree of interoperability. If the technologies are sufficiently diverse, then the attack propagation will be reduced or even stopped. As such, national asset managers are obliged to consider means for introducing diversity in a cost-effective manner to realize its security benefits (see Figure 1.7).

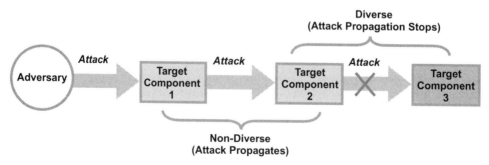

Figure 1.7 Introducing diversity to national infrastructure.

Diversity is especially tough to implement in national infrastructure for several reasons. First, it must be acknowledged that a single, major software vendor tends to currently dominate the personal computer (PC) operating system business landscape in most government and enterprise settings. This is not likely to change, so national infrastructure security initiatives must simply accept an ecosystem lacking in diversity in the PC landscape. The profile for operating system software on computer servers is slightly better from a diversity perspective, but the choices remain limited to a very small number of available sources. Mobile operating systems currently offer considerable diversity, but one cannot help but expect to see a trend toward greater consolidation.

Second, diversity conflicts with the often-found organizational goal of simplifying supplier and vendor relationships; that is, when a common technology is used throughout an organization, day-to-day maintenance, administration, and training costs are minimized. Furthermore, by purchasing in bulk, better terms are often available from a vendor. In contrast, the use of diversity could result in a reduction in the level of service provided in an organization. For example, suppose that an Internet service provider offers particularly secure and reliable network services to an organization. Perhaps the reliability is even measured to some impressive quantitative availability metric. If the organization is committed to diversity, then one might be forced to actually introduce a second provider with lower levels of reliability.

> Enforcing diversity of products and services might seem counterintuitive if you have a reliable provider.

In spite of these drawbacks, diversity carries benefits that are indisputable for large-scale infrastructure. One of the great challenges in national infrastructure protection will thus involve finding ways to diversify technology products and services without increasing costs and losing business leverage with vendors.

Consistency

The principle of *consistency* involves uniform attention to security best practices across national infrastructure components. Determining which best practices are relevant for which national asset requires a combination of local knowledge about the asset, as well as broader knowledge of security vulnerabilities in generic infrastructure protection. Thus, the most mature approach to consistency will combine compliance with relevant standards such as the Sarbanes–Oxley controls in the United States, with locally derived security policies that are tailored to the organizational mission. This implies that every organization charged with the design or operation of national infrastructure must have a local security policy. Amazingly, some large groups do not have such a policy today.

The types of best practices that are likely to be relevant for national infrastructure include well-defined software lifecycle methodologies, timely processes for patching software and systems, segregation of duty controls in system administration, threat management of all collected security information, security awareness training for all system administrators, operational configurations for infrastructure management, and use of software security tools to ensure proper integrity management. Most security experts agree on which best practices to include in a generic set of security requirements, as evidenced by the inclusion of a common core set of practices in every security standard. Attentiveness to consistency is thus one of the less controversial of our recommended principles.

The greatest challenge in implementing best practice consistency across infrastructure involves auditing. The typical audit process is performed by an independent third-party entity doing an analysis of target infrastructure to determine consistency with a desired standard. The result of the audit is usually a numeric score, which is then reported widely and used for management decisions. In the United States, agencies of the federal government are audited against a cyber security standard known as FISMA (Federal Information Security Management Act). While auditing does lead to improved best practice coverage, there are often problems. For example, many audits are done poorly, which results in confusion and improper management decisions. In addition, with all the emphasis on numeric ratings, many agencies focus more on their score than on good security practice.

> A good audit score is important but should not replace good security practices.

Today, organizations charged with protecting national infrastructure are subjected to several types of security audits. Streamlining these standards would certainly be a good idea, but some additional items for consideration include improving the types of common training provided to security administrators, as well as including past practice in infrastructure protection in common audit standards. The most obvious practical consideration for national infrastructure, however, would be national-level agreement on which standard or standards would be used to determine competence to protect national assets. While this is a straightforward concept, it could be tough to obtain wide concurrence among all national participants. A related issue involves commonality in national infrastructure operational configurations; this reduces the chances that a rogue configuration

> A national standard of competence for protecting our assets is needed.

installed for malicious purposes, perhaps by compromised insiders.

Depth

The principle of *depth* involves the use of multiple security layers of protection for national infrastructure assets. These layers protect assets from both internal and external attacks via the familiar "defense in depth" approach; that is, multiple layers reduce the risk of attack by increasing the chances that at least one layer will be effective. This should appear to be a somewhat sketchy situation, however, from the perspective of traditional engineering. Civil engineers, for example, would never be comfortable designing a structure with multiple flawed supports in the hopes that one of them will hold the load. Unfortunately, cyber security experts have no choice but to rely on this flawed notion, perhaps highlighting the relative immaturity of security as an engineering discipline.

One hint as to why depth is such an important requirement is that national infrastructure components are currently controlled by software, and everyone knows that the current state of software engineering is abysmal. Compared to other types of engineering, software stands out as the only one that accepts the creation of knowingly flawed products as acceptable. The result is that all nontrivial software has exploitable vulnerabilities, so the idea that one should create multiple layers of security defense is unavoidable. It is worth mentioning that the degree of diversity in these layers will also have a direct impact on their effectiveness (see Figure 1.8).

> Software engineering standards do not contain the same level of quality as civil and other engineering standards.

To maximize the usefulness of defense layers in national infrastructure, it is recommended that a combination of functional

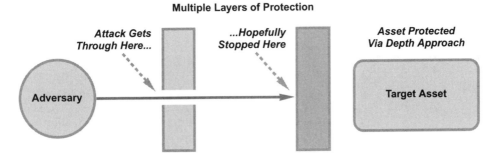

Multiple Layers of Protection

Attack Gets Through Here... ...*Hopefully Stopped Here* *Asset Protected Via Depth Approach*

Adversary

Target Asset

Figure 1.8 National infrastructure security through defense in depth.

and procedural controls be included. For example, a common first layer of defense is to install an access control mechanism for the admission of devices to the local area network. This could involve router controls in a small network or firewall access rules in an enterprise. In either case, this first line of defense is clearly functional. As such, a good choice for a second layer of defense might involve something procedural, such as the deployment of scanning to determine if inappropriate devices have gotten through the first layer. Such diversity will increase the chances that the cause of failure in one layer is unlikely to cause a similar failure in another layer.

A great complication in national infrastructure protection is that many layers of defense assume the existence of a defined network perimeter. For example, the presence of many flaws in enterprise security found by auditors is mitigated by the recognition that intruders would have to penetrate the enterprise perimeter to exploit these weaknesses. Unfortunately, for most national assets, finding a perimeter is no longer possible. The assets of a country, for example, are almost impossible to define within some geographic or political boundary, much less a network one. Security managers must therefore be creative in identifying controls that will be meaningful for complex assets whose properties are not always evident. The risk of getting this wrong is that in providing multiple layers of defense, one might misapply the protections and leave some portion of the asset base with no layers in place.

Discretion

The principle of *discretion* involves individuals and groups making good decisions to obscure sensitive information about national infrastructure. This is done by combining formal mandatory information protection programs with informal discretionary behavior. Formal mandatory programs have been in place for many years in the U.S. federal government, where documents are associated with classifications, and policy enforcement is based on clearances granted to individuals. In the most intense environments, such as top-secret compartments in the intelligence community, violations of access policies could be interpreted as espionage, with all of the associated criminal implications. For this reason, prominent breaches of highly classified government information are not common.

In commercial settings, formal information protection programs are gaining wider acceptance because of the increased need to protect personally identifiable information (PII) such as

> Naturally, top-secret information within the intelligence community is at great risk for attack or infiltration.

credit card numbers. Employees of companies around the world are starting to understand the importance of obscuring certain aspects of corporate activity, and this is healthy for national infrastructure protection. In fact, programs of discretion for national infrastructure protection will require a combination of corporate and government security policy enforcement, perhaps with custom-designed information markings for national assets. The resultant discretionary policy serves as a layer of protection to prevent national infrastructure-related information from reaching individuals who have no need to know such information.

A barrier in our recommended application of discretion is the maligned notion of "security through obscurity." Security experts, especially cryptographers, have long complained that obscurity is an unacceptable protection approach. They correctly reference the problems of trying to secure a system by hiding its underlying detail. Inevitably, an adversary discovers the hidden design secrets and the security protection is lost. For this reason, conventional computer security correctly dictates an open approach to software, design, and algorithms. An advantage of this open approach is the social review that comes with widespread advertisement; for example, the likelihood is low of software ever being correct without a significant amount of intense review by experts. So, the general computer security argument against "security through obscurity" is largely valid in most cases.

> "Security through obscurity" may actually leave assets more vulnerable to attack than an open approach would.

Nevertheless, any manager charged with the protection of nontrivial, large-scale infrastructure will tell you that discretion and, yes, obscurity are indispensable components in a protection program. Obscuring details around technology used, software deployed, systems purchased, and configurations managed will help to avoid or at least slow down certain types of attacks. Hackers often claim that by discovering this type of information about a company and then advertising the weaknesses they are actually doing the local security team a favor. They suggest that such advertisement is required to motivate a security team toward a solution, but this is actually nonsense. Programs around proper discretion and obscurity for infrastructure information are indispensable and must be coordinated at the national level.

Collection

The principle of *collection* involves automated gathering of system-related information about national infrastructure to enable security analysis. Such collection is usually done in real time and involves probes or hooks in applications, system software, network elements, or hardware devices that gather information of

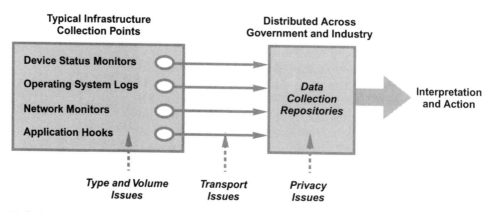

Figure 1.9 Collecting national infrastructure-related security information.

interest. The use of audit trails in small-scale computer security is an example of a long-standing collection practice that introduces very little controversy among experts as to its utility. Security devices such as firewalls produce log files, and systems purported to have some degree of security usefulness will also generate an audit trail output. The practice is so common that a new type of product, called a *security information management system* (SIMS), has been developed to process all this data.

The primary operational challenge in setting up the right type of collection process for computers and networks has been two-fold: First, decisions must be made about what types of information are to be collected. If this decision is made correctly, then the information collected should correspond to exactly the type of data required for security analysis, and nothing else. Second, decisions must be made about how much information is actually collected. This might involve the use of existing system functions, such as enabling the automatic generation of statistics on a router; or it could involve the introduction of some new type of function that deliberately gathers the desired information. Once these considerations are handled, appropriate mechanisms for collecting data from national infrastructure can be embedded into the security architecture (see Figure 1.9).

The technical and operational challenges associated with the collection of logs and audit trails are heightened in the protection of national assets. Because national infrastructure is so complex, determining what information should be collected turns out to be a difficult exercise. In particular, the potential arises with large-scale collection to intrude on the privacy of individuals and groups within a nation. As such, any initiative to protect infrastructure through the collection of data must include at least some measure of privacy policy determination. Similarly, the volumes of data collected from large infrastructure can exceed practical limits. Telecommunications collection systems designed to protect the integrity of a service provider backbone, for example, can easily generate many terabytes of data in hours of processing.

In both cases, technical and operational expertise must be applied to ensure that the appropriate data is collected in the proper amounts. The good news is that virtually all security protection algorithms require no deep, probing information of the type that might generate privacy or volumetric issues. The challenge arises instead when collection is done without proper advance analysis which often results in the collection of more data than is needed. This can easily lead to privacy problems in some national collection repositories, so planning is particularly necessary. In any event, a national strategy of data collection is required, with the usual sorts of legal and policy guidance on who collects what and under which circumstances. As we suggested above, this exercise must be guided by the requirements for security analysis—and nothing else.

> What and how much data to collect is an operational challenge.

> Only collect as much data as is necessary for security purposes.

Correlation

The principle of *correlation* involves a specific type of analysis that can be performed on factors related to national infrastructure protection. The goal of correlation is to identify whether security-related indicators might emerge from the analysis. For example, if some national computing asset begins operating in a sluggish manner, then other factors would be examined for a possible correlative relationship. One could imagine the local and wide area networks being analyzed for traffic that might be of an attack nature. In addition, similar computing assets might be examined to determine if they are experiencing a similar functional problem. Also, all software and services embedded in the national asset might be analyzed for known vulnerabilities. In each case, the purpose of the correlation is to combine and compare factors to help explain a given security issue. This type of comparison-oriented analysis is indispensable for national infrastructure because of its complexity.

> Monitoring and analyzing networks and data collection may reveal a hidden or emerging security threat.

Interestingly, almost every major national infrastructure protection initiative attempted to date has included a fusion center for real-time correlation of data. A fusion center is a physical security operations center with means for collecting and analyzing multiple sources of ingress data. It is not uncommon for such a center to include massive display screens with colorful,

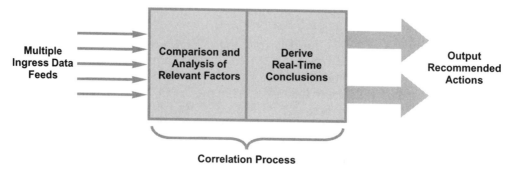

Figure 1.10 National infrastructure high-level correlation approach.

visualized representations, nor is it uncommon to find such centers in the military with teams of enlisted people performing the manual chores. This is an important point, because, while such automated fusion is certainly promising, best practice in correlation for national infrastructure protection must include the requirement that human judgment be included in the analysis. Thus, regardless of whether resources are centralized into one physical location, the reality is that human beings will need to be included in the processing (see Figure 1.10).

In practice, fusion centers and the associated processes and correlation algorithms have been tough to implement, even in small-scale environments. Botnets, for example, involve the use of source systems that are selected almost arbitrarily. As such, the use of correlation to determine where and why the attack is occurring has been useless. In fact, correlating geographic information with the sources of botnet activity has even led to many false conclusions about who is attacking whom. Countless hours have been spent by security teams poring through botnet information trying to determine the source, and the best one can

Three Steps to Improve Current Correlation Capabilities

1. The actual computer science around correlation algorithms needs to be better investigated. Little attention has been placed in academic computer science and applied mathematics departments to multifactor correlation of real-time security data. This could be changed with appropriate funding and grant emphasis from the government.
2. The ability to identify reliable data feeds needs to be greatly improved. Too much attention has been placed on *ad hoc* collection of volunteered feeds, and this complicates the ability for analysis to perform meaningful correlation.
3. The design and operation of a national-level fusion center must be given serious consideration. Some means must be identified for putting aside political and funding problems in order to accomplish this important objective.

hope for might be information about controllers or software drops. In the end, current correlation approaches fall short.

What is needed to improve present correlation capabilities for national infrastructure protection involves multiple steps.

Awareness

The principle of *awareness* involves an organization understanding the differences, in real time and at all times, between observed and normal status in national infrastructure. This status can include risks, vulnerabilities, and behavior in the target infrastructure. *Behavior* refers here to the mix of user activity, system processing, network traffic, and computing volumes in the software, computers, and systems that comprise infrastructure. The implication is that the organization can somehow characterize a given situation as being either normal or abnormal. Furthermore, the organization must have the ability to detect and measure differences between these two behavioral states. Correlation analysis is usually inherent in such determinations, but the real challenge is less the algorithms and more the processes that must be in place to ensure situational awareness every hour of every day. For example, if a new vulnerability arises that has impact on the local infrastructure, then this knowledge must be obtained and factored into management decisions immediately.

> Awareness builds on collection and correlation, but is not limited to those areas alone.

Managers of national infrastructure generally do not have to be convinced that situational awareness is important. The big issue instead is how to achieve this goal. In practice, real-time awareness requires attentiveness and vigilance rarely found in normal computer security. Data must first be collected and enabled to flow into a fusion center at all times so correlation can take place. The results of the correlation must be used to establish a profiled baseline of behavior so differences can be measured. This sounds easier than it is, because so many odd situations have the ability to mimic normal behavior (when it is really a problem) or a problem (when it really is nothing). Nevertheless, national infrastructure protection demands that managers of assets create a locally relevant means for being able to comment accurately on the state of security at all times. This allows for proper management decisions about security (see Figure 1.11).

Interestingly, situational awareness has not been considered a major component of the computer security equation to date. The concept plays no substantive role in small-scale security, such as in a home network, because when the computing base to be protected is simple enough, characterizing real-time situational status is just not necessary. Similarly, when a security manager puts in place security controls for a small enterprise, situational

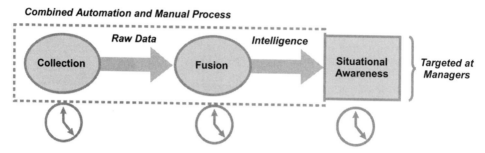

Figure 1.11 Real-time situation awareness process flow.

awareness is not the highest priority. Generally, the closest one might expect to some degree of real-time awareness for a small system might be an occasional review of system log files. So, the transition from small-scale to large-scale infrastructure protection does require a new attentiveness to situational awareness that is not well developed. It is also worth noting that the general notion of "user awareness" of security is also not the principle specified here. While it is helpful for end users to have knowledge of security, any professionally designed program of national infrastructure security must presume that a high percentage of end users will *always* make the wrong sorts of security decisions if allowed. The implication is that national infrastructure protection must never rely on the decision-making of end users through programs of awareness.

A further advance that is necessary for situational awareness involves enhancements in approaches to security metrics reporting. Where the non-cyber national intelligence community has done a great job developing means for delivering daily intelligence briefs to senior government officials, the cyber security community has rarely considered this approach. The reality is that, for situation awareness to become a structural component of national infrastructure protection, valid metrics must be developed to accurately portray status, and these must be codified into a suitable type of regular intelligence report that senior officials can use to determine security status. It would not be unreasonable to expect this cyber security intelligence to flow from a central point such as a fusion center, but in general this is not a requirement.

> Large-scale infrastructure protection requires a higher level of awareness than most groups currently employ.

Response

The principle of *response* involves assurance that processes are in place to react to any security-related indicator that becomes

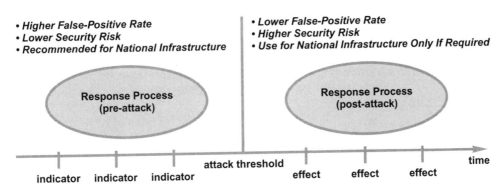

Figure 1.12 National infrastructure security response approach.

available. These indicators should flow into the response process primarily from the situational awareness layer. National infrastructure response should emphasize indicators rather than incidents. In most current computer security applications, the response team waits for serious problems to occur, usually including complaints from users, applications running poorly, and networks operating in a sluggish manner. Once this occurs, the response team springs into action, even though by this time the security game has already been lost. For essential national infrastructure services, the idea of waiting for the service to degrade before responding does not make logical sense.

An additional response-related change for national infrastructure protection is that the maligned concept of "false positive" must be reconsidered. In current small-scale environments, a major goal of the computer security team is to minimize the number of response cases that are initiated only to find that nothing was wrong after all. This is an easy goal to reach by simply waiting for disasters to be confirmed beyond a shadow of a doubt before response is initiated. For national infrastructure, however, this is obviously unacceptable. Instead, response must follow indicators, and the concept of minimizing false positives must not be part of the approach. The only quantitative metric that must be minimized in national-level response is risk (see Figure 1.12).

A challenge that must be considered in establishing response functions for national asset protection is that relevant indicators often arise long before any harmful effects are seen. This suggests that infrastructure protecting must have accurate situational awareness that considers much more than just visible impacts such as users having trouble, networks being down, or services being unavailable. Instead, often subtle indicators must

> A higher rate of false positives must be tolerated for national infrastructure protection.

be analyzed carefully, which is where the challenges arise with false positives. When response teams agree to consider such indicators, it becomes more likely that such indicators are benign. A great secret to proper incident response for national infrastructure is that higher false positive rates might actually be a good sign.

It is worth noting that the principles of collection, correlation, awareness, and response are all consistent with the implementation of a national fusion center. Clearly, response activities are often dependent on a real-time, ubiquitous operations center to coordinate activities, contact key individuals, collect data as it becomes available, and document progress in the response activities. As such, it should not be unexpected that national-level response for cyber security should include some sort of centralized national center. The creation of such a facility should be the centerpiece of any national infrastructure protection program and should involve the active participation of all organizations with responsibility for national services.

Implementing the Principles Nationally

To effectively apply this full set of security principles in practice for national infrastructure protection, several practical implementation considerations emerge:

- *Commissions and groups*—Numerous commissions and groups have been created over the years with the purpose of national infrastructure protection. Most have had some minor positive impact on infrastructure security, but none has had sufficient impact to reduce present national risk to acceptable levels. An observation here is that many of these commissions and groups have become the *end* rather than the *means* toward a cyber security solution. When this occurs, their likelihood of success diminishes considerably. Future commissions and groups should take this into consideration.
- *Information sharing*—Too much attention is placed on information sharing between government and industry, perhaps because information sharing would seem on the surface to carry much benefit to both parties. The advice here is that a comprehensive information sharing program is not easy to implement simply because organizations prefer to maintain a low profile when fighting a vulnerability or attack. In addition, the presumption that some organization—government or commercial—might have some nugget of information that could solve a cyber attack or reduce risk is not generally

consistent with practice. Thus, the motivation for a commercial entity to share vulnerability or incident-related information with the government is low; very little value generally comes from such sharing.

- *International cooperation*—National initiatives focused on creating government cyber security legislation must acknowledge that the Internet is global, as are the shared services such as the domain name system (DNS) that all national and global assets are so dependent upon. Thus, any program of national infrastructure protection must include provisions for international cooperation, and such cooperation implies agreements between participants that will be followed as long as everyone perceives benefit.
- *Technical and operational costs*—To implement the principles described above, considerable technical and operational costs will need to be covered across government and commercial environments. While it is tempting to presume that the purveyors of national infrastructure can simply absorb these costs into normal business budgets, this has not been the case in the past. Instead, the emphasis should be on rewards and incentives for organizations that make the decision to implement these principles. This point is critical because it suggests that the best possible use of government funds might be as straightforward as helping to directly fund initiatives that will help to secure national assets.

The bulk of our discussion in the ensuing chapters is technical in nature; that is, programmatic and political issues are conveniently ignored. This does not diminish their importance, but rather is driven by our decision to separate our concerns and focus in this book on the details of "what" must be done, rather than "how."

DECEPTION

Create a highly controlled network. Within that network, you place production systems and then monitor, capture, and analyze all activity that happens within that network Because this is not a production network, but rather our Honeynet, any traffic is suspicious by nature.

The Honeynet Project[1]

The use of deception in computing involves deliberately misleading an adversary by creating a system component that looks real but is in fact a trap. The system component, sometimes referred to as a *honey pot*, is usually functionality embedded in a computing or networking system, but it can also be a physical asset designed to trick an intruder. In both cases, a common interface is presented to an adversary who might access real functionality connected to real assets, but who might also unknowingly access deceptive functionality connected to bogus assets. In a well-designed deceptive system, the distinction between real and trap functionality should not be apparent to the intruder (see Figure 2.1).

The purpose of deception, ultimately, is to enhance security, so in the context of national infrastructure it can be used for large-scale protection of assets. The reason why deception works is that it helps accomplish any or all of the following four security objectives:

- *Attention*—The attention of an adversary can be diverted from real assets toward bogus ones.
- *Energy*—The valuable time and energy of an adversary can be wasted on bogus targets.

[1]The Honeynet Project, *Know Your Enemy: Revealing the Security Tools, Tactics, and Motives of the Blackhat Community*, Addison–Wesley Professional, New York, 2002. (I highly recommend this amazing and original book.) See also B. Cheswick and S. Bellovin, *Firewalls and Internet Security: Repelling the Wily Hacker*, 1st ed., Addison–Wesley Professional, New York, 1994; C. Stoll, *The Cuckoo's Egg: Tracking a Spy Through the Maze of Computer Espionage*, Pocket Books, New York, 2005.

Cyber Attacks. DOI: 10.1016/B978-0-12-384917-5.00002-0

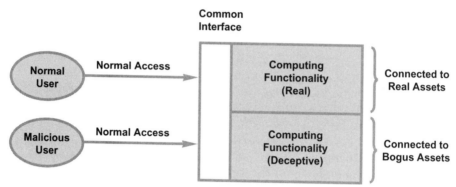

Common Interface

Normal User — Normal Access → Computing Functionality (Real) — Connected to Real Assets

Malicious User — Normal Access → Computing Functionality (Deceptive) — Connected to Bogus Assets

Figure 2.1 Use of deception in computing.

- *Uncertainty*—Uncertainty can be created around the veracity of a discovered vulnerability.
- *Analysis*—A basis can be provided for real-time security analysis of adversary behavior.

The fact that deception diverts the attention of adversaries, while also wasting their time and energy, should be familiar to anyone who has ever used a honey pot on a network. As long as the trap is set properly and the honey pot is sufficiently realistic, adversaries might direct their time, attention, and energy toward something that is useless from an attack perspective. They might even plant time bombs in trap functionality that they believe will be of subsequent use in targeting real assets. Obviously, in a honey pot, this is not the case. This type of deception is a powerful deterrent, because it defuses a cyber attack in a way that could fool an adversary for an extended period of time.

The possibility that deception might create uncertainty around the veracity of a discovered vulnerability has been poorly explored to date. The idea here is that when an intruder inevitably stumbles onto an exploitable hole it would be nice if that intruder were led to believe that the hole might be a trap. Thus, under the right circumstances, the intruder might actually choose to avoid exploitation of a vulnerability for fear that it has been intentionally planted. While this might seem difficult to implement in many settings, the concept is powerful because it allows security managers to defuse existing vulnerabilities *without even knowing about them*. This is a significant enough concept that it deserves repeating: The use of deception in computing allows system security managers to reduce the risk of vulnerabilities *that they might not even know are present*.

The fact that real-time analysis can be performed on a honey pot is reasonably well known in the computing community today.

> Deception is a powerful security tool, as it protects even unknown vulnerabilities.

Perhaps this is because it is a widely accepted best practice that security administrators should try to observe the behavior of intruders that have been detected. Most intrusion detection systems, for example, include threat management back-end systems that are designed to support such an objective. In the best case, the forensic analysis gathered during deception is sufficiently detailed to allow for identification of the adversary and possibly even prosecution. In the most typical case, however, accurate traceability to the original human source of a problem is rarely accomplished.

Luckily, the success of deceptive traps is assisted by the fact that intruders will almost always view designers and operators of national assets as being sloppy in their actions, deficient in their training, and incompetent in their knowledge. This extremely negative opinion of the individuals running national infrastructure is a core belief in virtually every hacking community in the world (and is arguably justified in some environments). Ironically, this low expectation is an important element that helps make stealth deception much more feasible, because honey pots do not always have to mimic a perfectly managed environment. Instead, adversaries can generally be led to find a system environment that is poorly administered, and they will not bat an eyelash. This helps the deception designer.

> Honey pots should not necessarily mimic perfect environments.

The less well-understood case of openly advertised deception relies on the adversary believing that designers and operators of national assets are competent enough to plant a believable trap into a national asset. This view represents a hurdle, because the hacking community will need to see convincing evidence before they will ever believe that anyone associated with a large organization would be competent enough to manage a complex program of deceptive computing. This is too bad, because open use of deception carries great advantages, as we will explain in more detail below. In any event, the psychology of understanding and managing adversary views is not straightforward. This soft issue must become part of the national infrastructure protection equation but will obviously require a new set of skills among security experts.

> Effective cyber deception involves understanding your adversary.

The most common implementation of deception involves the insertion of fake attack entry points, such as open service ports, that adversaries might expect to see in a normal system. The hope is that an adversary would discover (perhaps with a scanner) and then connect to these open service ports, which would in turn then lead to a honey pot. As suggested above, creating realism in a honey pot is not an easy task, but several design options do exist. One approach involves routing inbound open port connections to physically separate bogus systems that are isolated from real assets. This allows for a "forklift"-type copying

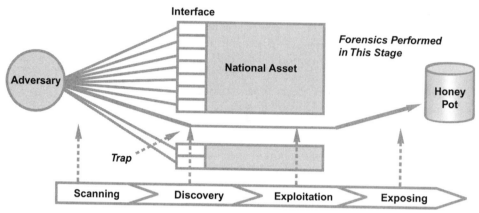

Figure 2.2 Stages of deception for national infrastructure protection.

of real functionality (perhaps with sensitive data sanitized) to an isolated, safe location where no real damage can be done.

Recall that, if the deception is advertised openly, the possibility arises that an adversary will not bother to attempt an attack. Admittedly, this scenario is a stretch, but the possibility does arise and is worth mentioning. Nevertheless, we will assume for the balance of this discussion that the adversary finds the deceptive entry point, presumes that it is real, and decides to move forward with an attack. If the subsequent deception is properly managed, then the adversary should be led down a controlled process path with four distinct attack stages: *scanning, discovery, exploitation,* and *exposing* (see Figure 2.2).

During the initial scanning stage, an adversary is searching through whatever means is available for exploitable entry points. The presumption in this stage is that the service interface includes trap functionality, such as bogus links on proxied websites that lead to a honey pot for collecting information. It is worth noting, however, that this "searching" process does not always imply the use of a network by an adversary. Instead, the adversary might be searching for exploitable entry points in contracts, processes, locked cabinets, safes, or even relationships with national infrastructure personnel. In practice, one might even expect a combination of computing and noncomputing searches for information about exploitable entry points. The deception must be designed accordingly.

During the discovery phase, an adversary finds an exploitable entry point, which might be real or fake. If the vulnerability is real, then one hopes that good back-end security is in place to avoid an infrastructure disaster. Nevertheless, the decision on the

Bear in mind that a cyber honey pot might require coordination with a tangible exploitable point outside the cyber world.

part of the intruder to exploit a discovered vulnerability, real or fake, is an important trigger point. Good infrastructure security systems would need to connect this exploitation point to a threat management system that would either open a security trouble ticket or would alert a security administrator that an intruder has either started an attack or fallen for the deceptive bait. Obviously, such alerts should not signal an intruder that a trap is present.

During the exploitation stage, the adversary makes use of the discovered vulnerability for whatever purposes they might have. If the vulnerability is real, then the usual infrastructure break-in scenario results. If the vulnerability is a trap, however, then its effectiveness will be directly related to the realism of the honey pot. For both stealth and non-stealth deception, this is the initial stage during which data becomes available for forensic analysis. A design consideration is that the actual asset must never become compromised as a result of the trap. This requirement will likely result in deceptive functionality running on computing "islands" that are functionally separated from the real assets.

> Actual assets must remain separate and protected so they are not compromised by a honey pot trap.

During the exposing stage in deception, adversary behavior becomes available for observation. Honey pots should include sufficient monitoring to expose adversary technique, intent, and identity. This is generally the stage during which management decisions are made about whether response actions are warranted. It is also a stage where real-time human actions are often required to help make the deceptive functionality look real. As we stated above, a great advantage that arises here is the low expectation the adversary will have regarding system administrative competency on the part of the infrastructure team. This allows the security team to use the excuse of poor setup to cover functional gaps that might exist in the deception.

> Monitoring honey pots takes security to the next level: potential for responsive action.

Any one of the four stages of deception can raise significant legal and social issues, so any program of national infrastructure protection must have participation from the national legal community to determine what is considered acceptable. The difference between a passive trap and an active lure, for example, is subtle and must be clarified before a live deployment is made into infrastructure. From a social perspective, one might hope that the acceptance that exists for using deception to catch online stalkers would be extended to the cyber security community for catching adversaries targeting national infrastructure.

Scanning Stage

In this first stage, the presumption is that an adversary is scanning whatever is available to find exploitation points to attack

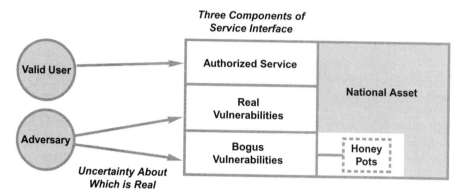

Figure 2.3 National asset service interface with deception.

national infrastructure. This scanning can include online searches for web-based information, network scans to determine port availability, and even offline searches of documents for relevant information. Deception can be used to divert these scanning attempts by creating false entry points with planted vulnerabilities. To deal with the offline case, the deception can extend to noncomputing situations such as intentionally leaving a normally locked cabinet or safe door open with bogus documents inserted to deceive a malicious insider.

The deceptive design goal during scanning is to make available an interface with three distinct components: *authorized services*, *real vulnerabilities*, and *bogus vulnerabilities*. In a perfect world, there would be no vulnerabilities, only authorized services. Unfortunately, given the extreme complexity associated with national infrastructure services, this is an unrealistic expectation, so real vulnerabilities will always be present in some way, shape, or form. When deception is used, these real vulnerabilities are complemented by fake ones and should be indistinguishable. Thus, an adversary will see three components when presented with a national asset interface with deception (see Figure 2.3).

Bogus vulnerabilities will generally be inserted based on the usual sorts of problems found in software. This is one of the few cases where the deficiencies of the software engineering discipline can actually be put to good use for security. One might imagine situations where new vulnerabilities are discovered and then immediately implemented as traps in systems that require protection. Nevertheless, planted holes do not always have to be based on such exploitable software bugs or system misconfigurations. In some cases, they might correspond to properly administered functionality, but that might not be considered acceptable for local use.

Honey Pots can be Built into Websites

A good example of a trap based on properly administered functionality might be a promiscuous tab on a website that openly solicits leaks of information; this is found sometimes on some of the more controversial blog sites. If legal and policy acceptance is given, then these links might be connected in a local proxied Intranet to a honey pot collection site. Insiders to an organization might then consider leaking information directly using this link to the seemingly valid Internet site, only to be duped into providing the leak to the local security team. Again, this should only be considered for deployment if all legal and policy requirements are met, but the example does help illustrate the possibilities.

A prominent goal of deception is to observe the adversary in action. This is done via real-time collection of data about intruder activity, along with reasoned analysis about intent. For example, if the intruder seems to be guessing passwords over and over again to gain access to a honey pot system, the administrator might decide in real time to simply grant access. A great challenge is that the automation possibilities of such response are not currently well understood and are barely included in security research programs. This is too bad, because such cases could really challenge and ultimately improve the skills of a good security administrator. One could even imagine national groups sponsoring contests between live intruders and live administrators who are battling against each other in real time in a contrived honey pot.

> Allowing an intruder access increases your risk level but also allows the security administrator to monitor the intruder's moves.

Deliberately Open Ports

Intruders routinely search the Internet for servers that allow connections to exploitable inbound services. These services are exploitable generally because they contain some weakness such as a buffer overflow condition that can be tripped to gain privileged access. Once privileged access is obtained, the intruder can perform administrative tasks such as changing system files, installing malware, and stealing sensitive information. All good system administrators understand the importance of *hardening* servers by disabling all exploitable and unnecessary services. The problem is that hardening is a complex process that is made more difficult in environments where the operating system is proprietary and less transparent. Amazingly, most software and server vendors still deliver their products in configurations that include most services being default enabled.

The deliberate insertion of open service ports on an Internet-facing server is the most straightforward of all deceptive computing

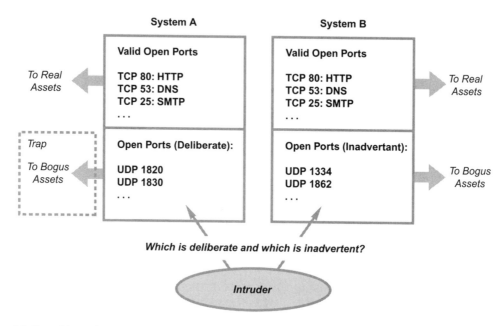

Figure 2.4 Use of deceptive open ports to bogus assets.

practices. The deliberately open ports are connected to back-end honey pot functionality, which is connected to monitoring systems for the purpose of observation and analysis. The result is that servers would thus present adversaries of national infrastructure with three different views of open service ports: (1) valid open ports one might expect, such as HTTP, DNS, and SMTP; (2) open ports that are inadvertently left open and might correspond to exploitable software; and (3) open ports that are deliberately inserted and connected to bogus assets in a honey pot. As long as it is generally understood that deception could *potentially* be deployed, there could be some uncertainty on the part of the adversary about which open ports are deliberate and which are inadvertent (see Figure 2.4).

Security managers who use port scanners as part of a normal program of enterprise network protection often cringe at this use of deception. What happens is that their scanners will find these open ports, which will result in the generation of reports that highlight the presumed vulnerabilities to managers, users, and auditors. Certainly, the output can be manually cropped to avoid such exposure, but this might not scale well to a large enterprise. Unfortunately, solutions are not easily identified that solve this incompatibility between the authorized use of port scanners and the deliberate use of open ports as traps. It represents yet another area for research and development in deceptive computing.

Another challenge is for security managers to knowingly keep open ports after running scanners that highlight these vulnerabilities.

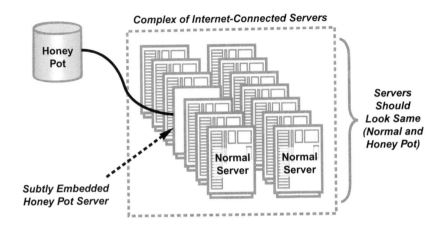

Figure 2.5 Embedding a honey pot server into a normal server complex.

An additional consideration with the deliberate use of open ports is that care must be taken on the back end to ensure that real assets cannot be exploited. Not surprisingly, practical techniques for doing this are not well known. For example, if the back-end deceptive software connected to deliberately open ports shares resources with valid assets, then the potential exists for negative side effects. The only reasonable approach today would involve deliberately open ports on bogus servers that are honey pots with no valid resources. These servers should be subtly embedded into server complexes so they look normal, but they should be hardwired to separate honey pot assets. This reduces the likelihood of negative side effects on normal servers (see Figure 2.5).

In practice, the real challenge to the deceptive use of open ports is creating port-connected functionality that is sufficiently valid to fool an expert adversary but also properly separated from valid services so no adversary could make use of the honey pot to advance an attack. Because computer science does not currently offer much foundational assistance in this regard, national infrastructure protection initiatives must include immediate programs of research and development to push this technique forward.

Discovery Stage

The discovery stage corresponds to the adversary finding and accepting the security bait embedded in the trap. The two corresponding security goals during this stage are to make an intruder believe that real vulnerabilities could be bogus and that bogus vulnerabilities could be real. The first of these goals is accomplished by making the deception program well-established and openly known. Specific techniques for doing this include the following:

- *Sponsored research*—The use of deception in national infrastructure could become generally presumed through the open sponsorship and funding of unclassified research and development work in this area.
- *Published case studies*—The open publication of case studies where deception has been used effectively in national asset protection increases the likelihood that an adversary might consider a found vulnerability to be deliberate.
- *Open solicitations*—Requests for Information (RFIs) and Requests for Proposals (RFPs) should be openly issued by national asset protectors. This implies that funding must be directed toward security projects that would actually use deceptive methods.

Interestingly, the potential that an adversary will hesitate before exploiting a real vulnerability increases only when the use of deception appears to be a real possibility. It would seem a hollow goal, for example, to simply announce that deception is being used without honest efforts to really deploy such deceptions in national infrastructure. This is akin to placing a home protection sign in the landscaping without ever installing a real security system. For openly advertised deception to work, the national infrastructure team must be fully committed to actually doing the engineering, deployment, and operation.

> Openly advertised use of deception may cause adversaries to question whether a discovered vulnerability is valid or bogus.

The second goal of making bogus vulnerabilities look real will be familiar to computer security experts who have considered the use of honey pots. The technique of duplication is often used in honey pot design, where a bogus system is a perfect copy of a real one but without the back-end connectivity to the real asset being protected. This is generally done by duplicating the front-end interface to a real system and placing the duplicate next to a back-end honey pot. Duplication greatly increases realism and is actually quite easy to implement in practice (see Figure 2.6).

As suggested above, the advantage of duplication in honey pot design is that it maximizes authenticity. If one finds, for example, a real vulnerability in some front-end server, then an image of that vulnerable server could be used in future deceptive configurations. Programs of national infrastructure protection should thus find ways to effectively connect vulnerability discovery processes to honey pot design. Thus, when a truly interesting vulnerability is found, it can become the front end to a future deceptive trap.

> Turn discovered vulnerabilities into advantages by mimicking them in honey pot traps.

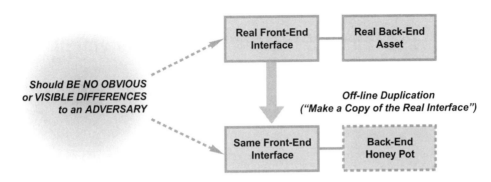

Figure 2.6 Duplication in honey pot design.

Deceptive Documents

The creation and special placement of deceptive documents is an example method for tricking adversaries during discovery. This technique, which can be done electronically or manually, is especially useful for detecting the presence of a malicious insider and will only work under two conditions:

- *Content*—The bogus document must include information that is convincingly realistic. Duplication of a valid document with changes to the most sensitive components is a straightforward means for doing this.
- *Protection*—The placement of the bogus document should include sufficient protections to make the document appear truly realistic. If the protection approach is thin, then this will raise immediate suspicion. Sabotage can be detected by protecting the bogus document in an environment that cannot be accessed by anyone other than trusted insiders.

An illustrative approach for national infrastructure protection would follow these steps: First, a document is created with information that references a specially created bogus asset, such as a phone number, physical location, or server. The information should never be real, but it should be very realistic. Next, the document is stored in a highly protected location, such as a locked safe (computer or physical). The presumption is that under normal circumstances the document should sit idly in the locked safe, as it should have no real purpose to anyone. Finally, the specially created bogus asset is monitored carefully for any attempted compromise. If someone finds and grabs the document, then one can conclude that some insider is not to be trusted.

Steps to Planting a Bogus Document

To effectively plant a bogus document, consider following these steps:

1. Create a file with instructions for obtaining what would appear to be extremely sensitive information. The file could include a phone number, an Internet address for a server, and perhaps a room location in some hotel.
2. Encrypt the file and store it on a server (or print and lock it in a safe) that one would presume to be protected from inside or outside access.
3. Put monitoring of the server or safe in place, with no expectation of a time limit. In fact, the monitoring might go on indefinitely, because one would expect to see no correlative behavior on these monitored assets (see Figure 2.7).

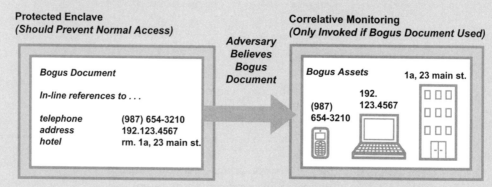

Figure 2.7 Planting a bogus document in a protected enclave.

It should be obvious that the example scheme shown in Figure 2.7 works as well for an electronic document protected by encryption and access control as for a manual paper document locked in a protected safe. In both cases, one would expect that no one would ever correlate these bogus references. If it turns out that the monitoring shows access to these bogus assets in some related way, then one would have to assume that the protected enclave has been compromised. (Monitoring a hotel might require complex logistics, such as the use of hidden cameras.) In any event, these assets would provide a platform for subsequent analysis of exploitation activity by the adversary.

Exploitation Stage

The third stage of the deception lifecycle for an adversary involves exploitation of a discovered vulnerability. This is a key

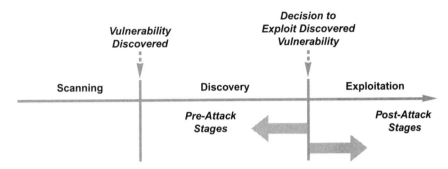

Figure 2.8 Pre- and post-attack stages at the exploitation stage.

step in the decision process for an adversary because it is usually the first stage in which policy rules or even laws are actually violated. That is, when an intruder begins to create a cyber attack, the initial steps are preparatory and generally do not violate any specific policy rules or laws. Sometimes security experts refer to this early activity as *low radar actions*, and when they are detected they are referred to as *indications and warnings*. Determining whether to respond to indications and warnings is a challenge, because response requires time and energy. If the track record of the security team involves many response actions to indications and warnings that are largely false positives, then the organization is often tempted to reduce the response trigger point. This is a bad idea for national infrastructure, because the chances increase that a real event will occur that is not responded to promptly.

Responding to a large number of false positives is necessary to adequately protect national infrastructure.

As such, the protection of national infrastructure should involve a mind shift away from trying to reduce false positive responses to indications and warnings. Instead, the goal should be to deal with all instances in which indication and warning actions would appear to be building up to the threshold at which exploitation begins. This is especially important, because this threshold marks the first stage during which real assets, if targeted, might actually be damaged (see Figure 2.8).

The key requirement at this decision point is that any exploitation of a bogus asset must not cause disclosure, integrity, theft, or availability problems with any real asset. Such non-interference between bogus and real assets is easiest to accomplish when these assets are kept as separate as possible. Physical separation of assets is straightforward; a real software application with real data, for example, could be separated from a bogus application with fake data by simply hosting each on different servers, perhaps even on different networks. This is how most honey pots operate, and the risk of interference is generally low.

Achieving noninterference in an environment where resources are shared between real and fake assets is more challenging. To accomplish this goal, the deception designer must be creative. For example, if some business process is to be shared by both real and fake functionality, then care must be taken by the deception operators to ensure that real systems are not degraded in any way. Very little research has been done in this area, especially for availability threats. Allowing a malicious adversary to execute programs on a live, valid system, for example, would provide opportunities for malicious resource exhaustion. Nevertheless, the general approach has considerable promise and deserves more attention.

> When bogus and real assets reside on the same server, vulnerability risk increases dramatically.

A related issue involves the possibility that intrusion detection and incident response systems might be fooled during exploitation into believing that trap functionality is real. White hat teams in companies have dealt with this problem for years, and they must coordinate with security teams to ensure that their activity does not cause a false alarm. This can be accomplished in several ways:

- *Process coordination*—This involves the honey pot team coordinating their activities in advance with the infrastructure security teams. The problem is that it tends to highlight the deception and might destroy some hidden transparency, especially if the deception is designed to detect malicious insiders.
- *Trap isolation*—This involves making certain that security systems, such as intrusion detection probes, are not in the deceptive path. Ongoing architectural analysis is required in this case to make sure that the condition holds throughout the system lifecycle.
- *Back-end insiders*—If the security team includes some trusted insiders involved in response activities, then they might be able to ensure that a response to deceptive action does not waste time and resources. This works best if the insider is a decision-maker.
- *Process allowance*—In this case, the detection and response activities are allowed to proceed. This is the recommended case if the deception is considered sensitive and must be totally hidden from insiders.

The exploitation stage is the most dangerous part of the deceptive lifecycle because it involves real malicious activity from an adversary. Infrastructure teams must learn to understand and respect the potential for real damage if this stage is not managed carefully.

Procurement Tricks

One way to understand adversary behavior is to compare it in different environments. An example involves a deception designer creating two separate supplier solicitations for a given product or service. One solicitation would be for a benign, noncritical, nonsensitive application; the other would be for an obviously sensitive, nationally critical application. In both cases, *exactly the same product or service* would be requested, but when they are delivered to each application detailed examination would be initiated to identify differences. Any differences found in the delivered product by the intentionally planted "critical buyer" and "benign buyer" would be viewed as potential exploits (see Figure 2.9).

The deception described above only works if sufficient forensic capability exists to compare the two delivered products. For any product or service, this could include comparison of relative software size, system performance, product documentation, service functionality, or technical support. One could even imagine a second level of deception using social engineering where an impassioned plea would be made to the supplier for some undocumented type of emergency support, usually remote administration. If either of the delivered products is set up for such remote administration, then the national asset manager would know that something is wrong.

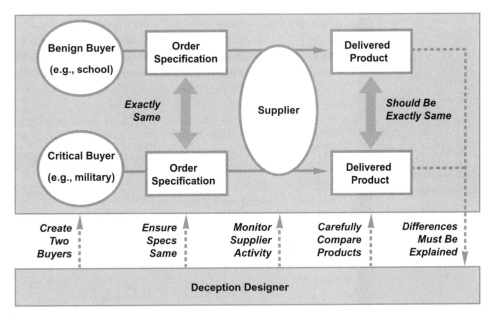

Figure 2.9 Using deception against malicious suppliers.

The procurement lifecycle is one of the most underestimated components in national infrastructure protection from an attack perspective. Generally, security teams focus on selecting, testing, installing, and operating functionality, with seemingly mundane procurement tasks left to the supply chain team. This is a huge mistake, and adversaries understand this point well. Thus, national infrastructure protection initiatives must extend to the procurement process, and the clever use of deception is a powerful tool in this regard.

> National infrastructure protection must extend from procurement to operating functionality in order to be truly effective.

Exposing Stage

The final stage in the deception lifecycle involves the adversary exposing behavior to the deception operator. Presumably, in this stage, the adversary is now hacking away at the trap functionality, convinced that all systems and assets are real. All sorts of possibilities arise in terms of how this hacking will proceed. It could be a flurry of intense activity in a short period of time or it could be a drawn-out process of low and slow actions, so the deception team must have patience. Also, during this stage, the adversary might expose the use of well-known hacking techniques and tools or, alternatively, could demonstrate use of techniques not previously seen by the security team (see Figure 2.10).

The challenge in this stage is that the deception must allow a window for observation of intruder activity, but must also be hidden. It must provide a convenient interface for the deception team to collect data but also must provide a way for commands to be issued or changes to be made in real time. Unfortunately, few commercial products exist that are designed to support these features. Specific functional requirements for the monitoring

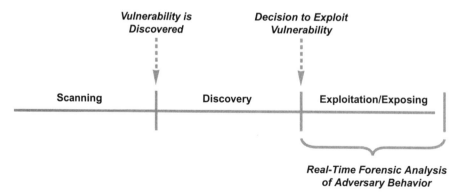

Figure 2.10 Adversary exposing stage during deception.

environment during the exposing stage of deception include the following:

- *Sufficient detail*—The monitoring environment must provide sufficient detail so the deception operator can determine what is going on. For example, overly cryptic audit logs in terse format with gaps in certain areas would not be the best approach. The usual administrative interface to an operating system (generally through a command interface) is often the most desirable approach. One should not expect fancy, colorful displays for the monitoring task because most security analysts prefer the convenience of a terse command line interface.
- *Hidden probes*—Monitoring in this stage of the deception works only if it is completely hidden. If an adversary figures out that someone is watching, then behavior modification would occur immediately. Simple tasks must therefore be implemented such as suppressed listing of any processes launched by the deception team (unless desired). The art of creating realistic functionality to hide probes requires support and nurturing in the security community.
- *Real-time observation*—The deception operator should have access to information about exposed behavior as it happens. The degree of real time for such monitoring (e.g., instantaneous, within seconds, within minutes) would depend on the local circumstances. In most cases, this observation is simply done by watching system logs, but more advanced tools are required to record and store information about intruder behavior.

As we suggested above, in all cases of deception monitoring the key design goal should be to ensure a believable environment. No suspicious or unexplainable processes should be present that could tip off an intruder that logging is ongoing. Fake audit logs are also a good way to create believability; if a honey pot is developed using an operating system with normal audit logging, then this should be enabled. A good adversary will likely turn it off. The idea is that hidden monitoring would have to be put in place underneath the normal logging—and this would be functionality that the adversary could not turn off.

> Observing intruder activity can be an informative but risky process during the exposure stage.

Interfaces Between Humans and Computers

The gathering of forensic evidence during the analysis of intruder behavior in a honey pot often relies on detailed understanding of how systems, protocols, and services interact. Specifically, this type of communication can be performed in four different ways: *human-to-human*, *human-to-computer*, *computer-to-human*, and

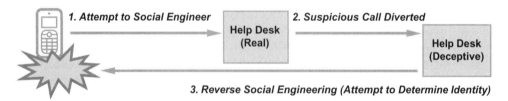

1. Attempt to Social Engineer

Help Desk
(Real)

2. Suspicious Call Diverted

Help Desk
(Deceptive)

3. Reverse Social Engineering (Attempt to Determine Identity)

Figure 2.11 Deceptively exploiting the human-to-human interface.

computer-to-computer. If we take the first term (human or computer) to mean the intruder and we take the second term to mean the honey pot manager, then we can make some logical distinctions.

First, it should be obvious that, in an automated attack such as a botnet, the real-time behavior of the attack system will not change based on some subjective observation of honey pot functionality. Certainly, the interpretation of the results of the botnet could easily affect the thinking of the botnet operator, but the real-time functionality is not going to be affected. As such, the most powerful cases in real-time forensic analysis of honey pot behavior will be the cases where human-to-human and human-to-computer interactions are being attempted by an intruder. Let's examine each in turn.

The most common human-to-human interaction in national infrastructure involves help desk or customer care support functions, and the corresponding attack approach involves social engineering of such activity. The current state of the art in dealing with this vulnerability is to train operators and customer care personnel to detect attempts at social engineering and to report them to the security team. Deception, however, introduces a more interesting option. If the likelihood is high that social engineering is being attempted, then an advanced approach to protection might involve deceiving the adversary into believing that they have succeeded. This can be accomplished quite easily by simply training operators to divert social engineering attempts to specially established help desks that are phony. The operators at these phony desks would reverse social engineer such attackers to get them to expose their identity or motivation (see Figure 2.11).

The most common human-to-computer interaction occurs when an intruder is trying to gain unauthorized access through a series of live, interactive commands. The idea is that intruders should be led to believe that their activity is invoking services on the target system, as in the usual type of operating system hacking. A good example might involve an intruder repeatedly trying to execute some command or operation in a trap system. If

> Real-time forensic analysis is not possible for every scenario, such as a botnet attack.

the security team notices this intent and can act quickly enough, the desired command or operation could be deliberately led to execute. This is a tricky engagement, because an expert adversary might notice that the target configuration is changing, which obviously is not normal.

> An expert adversary may become aware of the security team observing the attempted intrusion.

National Deception Program

One might hope that some sort of national deception program could be created based on a collection of traps strategically planted across national infrastructure components, tied together by some sort of deception analysis backbone. Such an approach is unlikely, because deception remains a poorly understood security approach, and infrastructure managers would be very hesitant to allow traps to be implanted in production systems. These traps, if they malfunction or do not work as advertised, could trick authorized users or impede normal operations.

Any realistic assessment of current security and information technology practice suggests that large-scale adoption of deception for national infrastructure protection would not be widely accepted today. As a result, programs of national deception would be better designed based on the following assumptions:

- *Selective infrastructure use*—One must assume that certain infrastructure components are likely to include deceptive traps but that others will not. At the time of this writing, many infrastructure teams are still grappling with basic computer security concepts; the idea that they would agree to install traps is not realistic. As such, any program of national deception must assume that not all components would utilize honey pots in the same manner.
- *Sharing of results and insights*—Programs of national deception can and should include a mechanism for the sharing of results and insights gained through operational use of traps and honey pots. Certainly, insight obtained through forensic analysis of adversary behavior can be shared in a structured manner.
- *Reuse of tools and methods*—National deception programs could serve as means for making honey pot and trap software available for deployment. In some cases, deception tools and methods that work in one infrastructure area can be reused in another.

The most common criticism of deception in large-scale national security is that automated tools such as botnets are not affected by trap functionality. While it is true that botnets attack infrastructure in a blindly automated manner regardless of whether the target is real or fake, the possibility remains that trap functionality might have some positive impact. A good example might be national coordination of numerous bogus endpoints that might be ready and willing to accept botnet software. If these endpoints are designed properly, one could imagine them being deliberately designed to mess up the botnet communication, perhaps by targeting the controllers themselves. This approach is often referred to as a *tarpit,* and one might imagine this method being quite interesting for degrading the effectiveness of a botnet.

SEPARATION

A limitation of firewalls is that they can only be as good as their access controls and filters. They might fail to detect subversive packets. In some situations, they might be bypassed altogether. For example, if a computer behind a firewall has a dial-up port, as is all too common, an intruder can get access by dialing the machine.

Dorothy Denning[1]

The separation of network assets from malicious intruders using a firewall is perhaps the most familiar protection approach in all of computer security. Today, you will find some sort of firewall deployed in or around virtually every computer, application, system, and network in the world. They serve as the centerpiece in most organizations' security functionality, including intrusion detection, antivirus filtering, and even identity management. An enormous firewall industry has emerged to support such massive deployment and use, and this industry has done nothing but continue to grow for years and years.

In spite of this widespread adoption, firewalls as separation mechanisms for large-scale infrastructure have worked to only a limited degree. The networks and systems associated with national infrastructure assets tend to be complex, with a multitude of different entry points for intruders through a variety of Internet service providers. In addition, the connectivity requirements for complex networks often result in large rule sets that permit access for many different types of services and source addresses. Worse, the complexity of large-scale networks often leads to unknown, unprotected entry points into and out of the enterprise (see Figure 3.1).

> Firewalls are valuable and frequently employed but may not provide enough protection to large-scale networks.

Certainly, the use of traditional perimeter firewalls will continue to play a role in the protection of national assets, as we will describe below. Egress filtering, for example, is often most efficiently performed at the perceived perimeter of an organization. Similarly, when two or more organizations share a private

---

[1] D. Denning, *Information Warfare and Security*, Addison–Wesley, New York, 1999, p. 354.

Cyber Attacks. DOI: 10.1016/B978-0-12-384917-5.00003-2

51

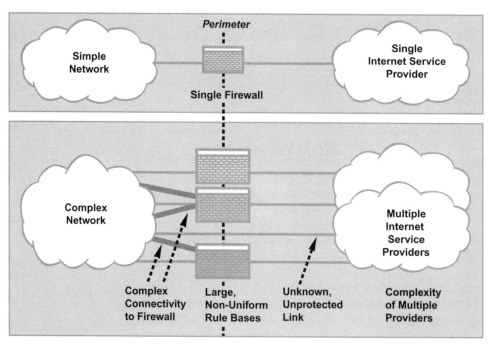

Figure 3.1 Firewalls in simple and complex networks.

connection, the connection endpoints are often the most natural place to perform firewall filtering, especially if traditional circuit-switched connections are involved. To achieve optimal separation in the protection of large-scale national assets, however, three new firewall approaches will be required:

- *Network-based separation*—Because the perimeter of any complex national infrastructure component will be difficult to define accurately, the use of separation methods such as network-based firewalls is imperative. Such cloud-based functionality allows a broader, more accurate view of the egress and ingress activity for an organization. It also provides a richer environment for filtering high-capacity attacks. The filtering of denial of service attacks aimed at infrastructure, for example, can only be stopped with special types of cloud-based filtering firewalls strategically placed in the network.

- *Internal separation*—National infrastructure protection will require a program of internal asset separation using firewalls strategically placed in infrastructure. This type of separation of internal assets using firewalls or other separation mechanisms (such as operating system access controls) is not generally present in most infrastructure environments. Instead, the idea persists that insiders should have unrestricted access to internal resources and that perimeter firewalls should protect resources from untrusted, external access. This model breaks down in complex infrastructure environments because it is so easy to plant insiders or penetrate complex network perimeters.

- *Tailored separation*—With the use of specialized protocols in national infrastructure management, especially supervisory control and data acquisition (SCADA), tailoring firewalls to handle unique protocols and services is a requirement. This is a challenge because commercial firewalls are generally designed for generic use in a wide market and tailoring will require a more focused effort. The result will be more accurate firewall operation without the need to open large numbers of service ports to enable SCADA applications.

> Commercially available firewalls are not designed for the large-scale complexity of our national infrastructure networks.

The reader might be amused to consider the irony presented today by network connectivity and security separation. Twenty years ago, the central problem in computer networking involved the rampant interoperability that existed between systems. Making two computers connect over a network was a significant challenge, one that computer scientists worked hard to overcome. In some instances, large projects would be initiated with the goal of connecting systems together over networks. Amazingly, the challenge we deal with today is not one of connectivity, but rather one of separation. This comes from the ubiquity of the Internet Protocol (IP), which enables almost every system on the planet to be connected with trivial effort. Thus, where previously we did not know how to interconnect systems, today we don't know how to separate them!

> Now that we are able to connect systems with ease, we must learn to separate them for protection!

What Is Separation?

In the context of national infrastructure protection, separation is viewed as a technique that accomplishes one of the following security objectives:

- *Adversary separation*—The first separation goal involves separating an asset from an adversary to reduce the risk of direct attack. Whatever implementation is chosen should result in the intruder having no direct means for accessing national assets.
- *Component distribution*—The second separation goal involves architecturally separating components in an infrastructure to distribute the risk of compromise. The idea here is that a compromise in one area of infrastructure should not be allowed to propagate directly.

The access restrictions that result from either of these separation approaches can be achieved through functional or physical means. Functional means involve software, computers, and networks, whereas physical means include tangible separations such as locks, safes, and cabinets. In practice, most separation access restrictions must be designed to focus on either the insider or outsider threat. The relationship between these different separation options can be examined based on the three primary factors involved in the use of separation for protecting infrastructure (see box).

A Working Taxonomy of Separation Techniques

The three primary factors involved in the use of separation for protecting infrastructure include the source of the *threat* (insider or outsider), the *target* of the security control (adversary or asset), and the *approach* used in the security control (functional or physical). We can thus use these three factors to create a separation taxonomy that might help to compare and contrast the various options for separating infrastructure from adversaries (see Figure 3.2).

The first column in the taxonomy shows that separation controls are focused on keeping either insiders or outsiders away from some asset. The key difference here is that insiders would typically be more trusted and would have more opportunity to gain special types of access. The second column indicates that the separation controls are focused on either keeping an adversary away from some asset or inherently separating components of the actual asset, perhaps through distribution. The third column identifies whether the separation approach uses computing functionality or would rely instead on some tangible, physical control.

Threat	Target	Approach	Example	
Insider	Adversary	Functional	Internal access control	Functional Adversary Techniques
Outsider	Adversary	Functional	Internet-facing firewall	
Insider	Asset	Functional	Application separation	Functional Asset Techniques
Outsider	Asset	Functional	Application distribution	
Insider	Adversary	Physical	Project compartmentalization	Physical Adversary and Asset Techniques
Outsider	Adversary	Physical	Information classification	
Insider	Asset	Physical	Internal network diversity	
Outsider	Asset	Physical	Physical host distribution	

Figure 3.2 Taxonomy of separation techniques.

From the first two rows of the taxonomy, it should be clear that internal access controls demonstrate a functional means for separating insider adversaries from an asset, whereas Internet firewalls achieve roughly the same end for outside adversaries. These firewalls might be traditional devices, as one might find in an enterprise, or special filtering devices placed in the network to throttle volume attacks. The third and fourth rows show that logical separation of an application is a good way to complicate an insider attack; this is comparably done for outsiders by distributing the application across different Internet-facing hosts. The last four rows in Figure 3.2 demonstrate different ways to use physical means to protect infrastructure, ranging from keeping projects and people separate from an asset to maintaining diversity and distribution of infrastructure assets. The following sections provide more detail on these separation taxonomy elements.

Functional Separation

Functional separation of an adversary from any computing asset is most commonly achieved using an access control mechanism with the requisite authentication and identity management. Access controls define which users can perform which actions on which entities. The access rules should be predetermined in a security policy. They should specify, for example, which users can access a given application, and, obviously, the validation of user identity must be accurate. In some cases, security policy rules must be more dynamic, as in whether a new type of traffic stream is allowed to proceed to some Internet ingress point. This might be determined by real-time analysis of the network flow.

An access policy thus emerges for every organization that identifies desired allowances for users requesting to perform actions on system entities. Firewall policies are the most common example of this; for example, users trying to connect to a web server might be subjected to an access control policy that would determine if this was to be permitted. Similarly, the IP addresses of some organization might be keyed into a firewall rule to allow access to some designated system. A major problem that occurs in practice with firewalls is that the rule base can grow to an enormous size, with perhaps thousands of rules. The result is complexity and a high potential for error. National infrastructure initiatives must identify rewards and incentives for organizations to keep their firewall rule bases as small as possible. Some organizations have used optimization tools for this purpose, and this practice should be encouraged for national assets.

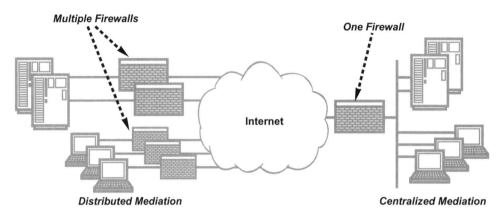

Figure 3.3 Distributed versus centralized mediation.

> In large networks, firewall rules can become so numerous that they actually increase the margin for error.

Two broad categories of security can be followed when trying to achieve functional separation of adversaries from any type of national infrastructure assets. The first involves distributing the responsibility for access mediation to the owners of smaller asset components such as individual computers or small networks; the second involves deployment of a large, centralized mediation mechanism through which all access control decisions would be made (see Figure 3.3).

The distributed approach has had considerable appeal for the global Internet community to date. It avoids the problem of having to trust a large entity with mediation decisions, it allows for commercial entities to market their security tools on a large scale to end users, and it places control of access policy close to the asset, which presumably should increase the likelihood that the policy is appropriate. The massive global distribution of computer security responsibility to every owner of a home personal computer is an example of this approach. End users must decide how to protect their assets, rather than relying on some centralized authority.

Unfortunately, in practice, the distributed approach has led to poor results. Most end users are unqualified to make good decisions about security, and even if a large percentage make excellent decisions, the ones who do not create a big enough vulnerability as to place the entire scheme at risk. Botnets, for example, prey on poorly managed end-user computers on broadband connections. When a home computer is infected with malware, there really is no centralized authority for performing a cleansing function. This lack of centralization on the Internet thus results in a huge security risk. Obviously, the Internet will never be redesigned to include centralized control; that would be impractical, if not impossible.

For national infrastructure, however, the possibility does exist for more centralized control. The belief here is that an increased reliance on centralized protection, especially in conjunction with the network service provider, will improve overall national asset protection methods. This does not imply, however, that distributed protection is not necessary. In fact, in most environments, skilled placement of both centralized and distributed security will be required to avoid national infrastructure attack.

> Centralized control versus multiple, independent firewalls—both have their advantages, so which is best for national infrastructure?

National Infrastructure Firewalls

The most common application of a firewall involves its placement between a system or enterprise to be protected and some untrusted network such as the Internet. In such an arrangement for the protection of a national asset, the following two possibilities immediately arise:

- *Coverage*—The firewall might not cover all paths between the national asset to be protected and the untrusted network such as the Internet. This is a likely case given the general complexity associated with most national infrastructure.
- *Accuracy*—The firewall might be forced to allow access to the national asset in a manner that also provides inadvertent, unauthorized access to certain protected assets. This is common in large-scale settings, especially because specialized protocols such as those in SCADA systems are rarely supported by commercial firewalls. As a result, the firewall operator must compensate by leaving certain ports wide open for ingress traffic.

To address these challenges, the design of national security infrastructure requires a skillful placement of separation functionality to ensure that all relevant traffic is mediated and that no side effects occur when access is granted to a specific asset. The two most effective techniques include aggregation of protections in the wide area network and segregation of protections in the local area network (see Figure 3.4).

Aggregating firewall functionality at a defined gateway is not unfamiliar to enterprise security managers. It helps ensure coverage of untrusted connections in more complex environments. It also provides a means for focusing the best resources, tools, and staff to one aggregated security complex. Segregation in a local area network is also familiar, albeit perhaps less practiced. It is effective in reducing the likelihood that external access to System A has the side effect of providing external access to System B. It requires management of more devices and does

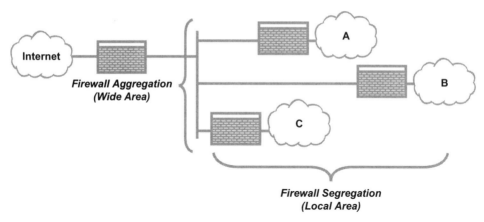

Figure 3.4 Wide area firewall aggregation and local area firewall segregation.

generally imply higher cost. Nevertheless, both of these techniques will be important in national infrastructure firewall placement.

A major challenge to national infrastructure comes with the massive increase in wireless connectivity that must be presumed for all national assets in the coming years. Most enterprise workers now carry around some sort of smart device that is ubiquitously connected to the Internet. Such smart devices have begun to resemble computers in that they can support browsing, e-mail access, and even virtual private network (VPN) access to applications that might reside behind a firewall. As such, the ease with which components of infrastructure can easily bypass defined firewall gateways will increase substantially. The result of this increased wireless connectivity, perhaps via 4G deployment, will be that all components of infrastructure will require some sort of common means for ensuring security.

Massive distribution of security to smart wireless endpoint devices may not be the best option, for all the reasons previously cited. It would require massive distribution, again, of the security responsibility to all owners of smart devices. It also requires vigilance on the part of every smart device owner, and this is not a reasonable expectation. An alternative approach involves identifying a common transport infrastructure to enforce desired policy. This might best be accomplished via the network transport carrier. Network service providers offer several advantages with regard to centralized security:

- *Vantage point*—The network service provider has a wide vantage point that includes all customers, peering points, and

> Effective protection of national infrastructure will undoubtedly be expensive due to the increased management of devices.

> Smart devices have added another layer of complexity to network protection.

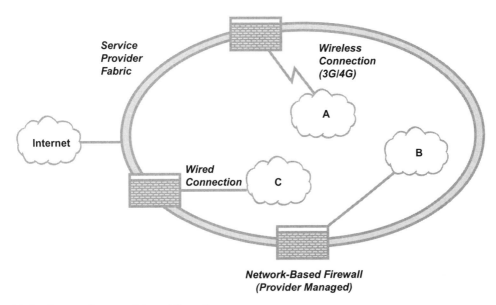

Figure 3.5 Carrier-centric network-based firewall.

gateways. Thus, if some incident is occurring on the Internet, the service provider will observe its effects.

- *Operations*—Network service providers possess the operational capability to ensure up-to-date coverage of signatures, updates, and new security methods, in contrast to the inability of most end users to keep their security software current.

- *Investment*—Where most end users, including enterprise groups, are unlikely to have funds sufficient to install multiple types of diverse or even redundant security tools, service providers can often support a business case for such investment.

For these reasons, a future view of firewall functionality for national infrastructure will probably include a new aggregation point—namely, the concept of implementing a network-based firewall in the cloud (see Figure 3.5).

> A firewall in the cloud may be the future of firewall functionality.

In the protection of national infrastructure, the use of network-based firewalls that are embedded in service provider fabric will require a new partnership between carriers and end-user groups. Unfortunately, most current telecommunications service level agreements (SLAs) are not compatible with this notion, focusing instead on packet loss and latency issues, rather than policy enforcement. This results in too many current cases of a national infrastructure provider being attacked, with the service provider offering little or no support during the incident.

Obviously, this situation must change for the protection of national assets.

DDOS Filtering

A major application of the network-based firewall concept includes a special type of mediation device embedded in the wide area network for the purpose of throttling distributed denial of service (DDOS) attacks. This device, which can be crudely referred to as a *DDOS filter*, is essential in modern networking, given the magnified risk of DDOS attacks from botnets. Trying to filter DDOS attacks at the enterprise edge does not make sense given the physics of network ingress capacity. If, for example, an enterprise has a 1-Gbps ingress connection from the Internet, then a botnet directing an inbound volume of anything greater than 1 Gbps will overwhelm the connection.

> The risk of DDOS attacks must be effectively addressed.

The solution to this volume problem is to move the filtering upstream into the network. Carrier infrastructure generally provides the best available option here. The way the filtering would work is that volumetric increases in ingress traffic would cause a real-time redirection of traffic to a DDOS filtering complex charged with removing botnet-originating traffic from valid traffic. Algorithms for performing such filtering generally key on the type of traffic being sent, the relative size of the traffic, and any other hint that might point to the traffic being of an attack nature. Once the traffic has been filtered, it is then funneled to the proper ingress point. The result is like a large safety valve or shock absorber in the wide area network that turns on when an attack is under way toward some target enterprise (see Figure 3.6).

> Moving the filtering functionality into the network will allow legitimate traffic to pass through and the discovery of potential DDOS attacks.

Quantitative analysis associated with DDOS protection of national infrastructure is troubling. If, for example, we assume that bots can easily steal 500 Kbps of broadband egress from the unknowing infected computer owner, then it would only require three bots to overwhelm a T1 (1.5-Mbps) connection. If one carries out this argument, then botnets with 16,000 bots are sufficient to overwhelm a 10-Gbps connection. Given the existence of prominent botnets such as Storm and Conficker, which some experts suggest could have as many as 2 or 3 million bots, the urgency associated with putting DDOS filtering in place cannot be understated. An implication is that national infrastructure protection initiatives must include some measure of DDOS filtering to reduce the risk of DDOS attacks on national assets.

A serious problem that must be addressed, however, in current DDOS attacks on infrastructure involves a so-called

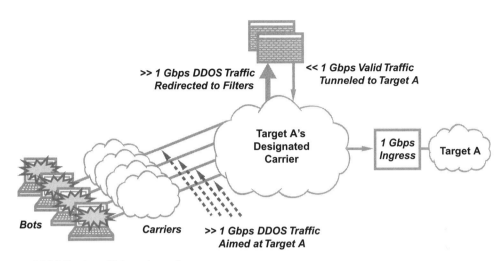

Figure 3.6 DDOS filtering of inbound attacks on target assets.

amplification approach. Modern DDOS attacks are generally designed in recognition of the fact that DDOS filters exist to detect large inbound streams of unusual traffic. Thus, to avoid inbound filtering in carrier infrastructure, adversaries have begun to follow two design heuristics. First, they design DDOS traffic to mimic normal system behavior, often creating transactions that look perfectly valid. Second, they design their attack to include small inbound traffic that utilizes some unique aspect of the target software to create larger outbound responses. The result is a smaller, less obvious inbound stream which then produces much larger outbound response traffic that can cause the DDOS condition.

> Modern DDOS attacks take into account a more advanced filtering system and thus design the DDOS traffic accordingly.

The Great Challenge of Filtering Out DDOS Attacks

The great challenge regarding current DDOS attacks is that the only way to avoid the sort of problem mentioned in the text is through nontrivial changes in target infrastructure. Two of these nontrivial changes are important to mention here:

1. Stronger authentication of inbound inquiries and transactions from users is imperative. This is not desirable for e-commerce sites designed to attract users from the Internet and also designed to minimize any procedures that might scare away customers.

2. To minimize the amplification effects of some target system, great care must go into analyzing the behavior of Internet-visible applications to determine if small inquiries can produce much larger responses. This is particularly important for public shared services such as the domain name system, which is quite vulnerable to amplification attacks.

These types of technical considerations *must* be included in modern national infrastructure protection initiatives.

SCADA Separation Architecture

Many critical national infrastructure systems include supervisory control and data acquisition (SCADA) functionality. These systems can be viewed as the set of software, computers, and networks that provide remote coordination of controls systems for tangible infrastructures such as power generation systems, chemical plants, manufacturing equipment, and transportation systems. The general structure of SCADA systems includes the following components:

- *Human-machine interface (HMI)*—The interface between the human operator and the commands relevant to the SCADA system
- *Master terminal unit (MTU)*—The client system that gathers data locally and transmits it to the remote terminal unit
- *Remote terminal unit (RTU)*—The server that gathers data remotely and sends control signals to field control systems
- *Field control systems*—Systems that have a direct interface to field data elements such as sensors, pumps, and switches

The primary security separation issue in a SCADA system architecture is that remote access from an MTU to a given RTU must be properly mediated according to a strong access control policy.[2] The use of firewalls between MTUs and RTUs is thus imperative in any SCADA system architecture. This separation must also enforce policy from any type of untrusted network, such as the Internet, into the RTUs. If this type of protection is not present, then the obvious risk emerges that an adversary can remotely access and change or influence the operation of a field control system.

> Remote access from MTUs to RTUs opens the door for adversaries to take advantage of this separation.

As one might expect, all the drawbacks associated with large-scale firewall deployment are also present in SCADA systems. Coverage and accuracy issues must be considered, as well as the likelihood that individual components have direct or wireless connections to the Internet through unknown or unapproved channels. This implies that protection of RTUs from unauthorized access will require a combination of segregated local area firewalls, aggregated enterprise-wide firewalls, and carrier-hosted network-based firewalls (see Figure 3.7).

The biggest issue for SCADA separation security is that most of the associated electromechanical systems were designed and evolved in an environment largely separate from conventional computing and networking. Few computing texts explain the subtle details in SCADA system architecture; in fact, computer scientists can easily complete an advanced program of study without the slightest exposure to SCADA issues. Thus, in far too many

[2]R. Krutz, *Securing SCADA Systems*, John Wiley & Sons, New York, 2006.

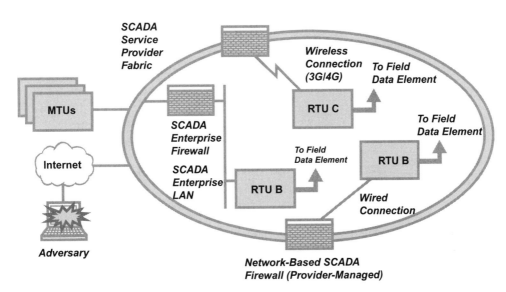

Figure 3.7 Recommended SCADA system firewall architecture.

SCADA environments, the computerized connections between tangible systems and their control networks have occurred in an *ad hoc* manner, often as a result of establishing local convenience such as remote access. For this reason, the likelihood is generally low that state-of-the-art protection mechanisms are in place to protect a given SCADA system from cyber attack.

> Protection mechanisms must be updated to effectively protect a SCADA system from cyber attack.

An additional problem that emerges for SCADA firewall usage is that commercial firewalls do not generally support SCADA protocols. When this occurs, the firewall operator must examine which types of ports are required for usage of the protocol, and these would have to be opened. Security experts have long known that one of the great vulnerabilities in a network is the inadvertent opening of ports that can be attacked. Obviously, national infrastructure protection initiatives must be considered that would encourage and enable new types of firewall functionality such as special proxies that could be embedded in SCADA architecture to improve immediate functionality.

> Opening ports, although necessary, is a risky endeavor, as it subjects the SCADA system to increased vulnerabilities.

Physical Separation

One separation technique that is seemingly obvious, but amazingly underrepresented in the computer security literature, is the physical isolation of one network from another. On the surface, one would expect that nothing could be simpler for separating one network from any untrusted environment than just unplugging all external connections. The process is known as

> Air gapping allows for physical separation of the network from untrusted environments.

> As a company grows, physical separation as a protection feature becomes increasingly complex.

air gapping, and it has the great advantage of not requiring any special equipment, software, or systems. It can be done to separate enterprise networks from the Internet or components of an enterprise network from each other.

The problem with physical separation as a security technique is that as complexity increases in some system or network to be isolated, so does the likelihood that some unknown or unauthorized external connection will arise. For example, a small company with a modest local area network can generally enjoy high confidence that external connections to the Internet are well known and properly protected. As the company grows, however, and establishes branch offices with diverse equipment, people, and needs, the likelihood that some generally unrecognized external connectivity will arise is high. Physical separation of network thus becomes more difficult.

So how does one go about creating a truly air-gapped network? The answer lies in the following basic principles:

- *Clear policy*—If a network is to be physically isolated, then clear policy must be established around what is and what is not considered an acceptable network connection. Organizations would thus need to establish policy checks as part of the network connection provision process.
- *Boundary scanning*—Isolated networks, by definition, must have some sort of identifiable boundary. Although this can certainly be complicated by firewalls embedded in the isolated network, a program of boundary scanning will help to identify leaks.
- *Violation consequences*—If violations occur, clear consequences should be established. Government networks in the U.S. military and intelligence communities, such as SIPRNet and Intelink, are protected by laws governing how individuals must use these classified networks. The consequences of violation are not pleasant.
- *Reasonable alternatives*—Leaks generally occur in an isolated network because someone needs to establish some sort of communication with an external environment. If a network connection is not a reasonable means to achieve this goal, then the organization must provide or support a reasonable work-around alternative.

Perhaps the biggest threat to physical network isolation involves dual-homing a system to both an enterprise network and some external network such as the Internet. Such dual-homing can easily arise where an end user utilizes the same system to access both the isolated network and the Internet. As laptops have begun to include native 3G wireless access, this likelihood of dual-homing increases. Regardless of the method, if any

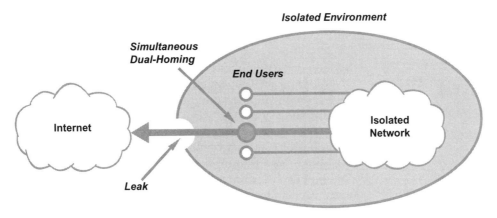

Figure 3.8 Bridging an isolated network via a dual-homing user.

sort of connectivity is enabled simultaneously to both systems, then the end user creates an inadvertent bridge (see Figure 3.8).

It is worth mentioning that the bridge referenced above does not necessarily have to be established simultaneously. If a system connects to one network and is infected with some sort of malware, then this can be spread to another network upon subsequent connectivity. For this reason, laptops and other mobile computing devices need to include some sort of native protection to minimize this problem. Unfortunately, the current state of the art for preventing malware downloads is poor.

A familiar technique for avoiding bridges between networks involves imposing strict policy on end-user devices that can be used to access an isolated system. This might involve preventing certain laptops, PCs, and mobile devices from being connected to the Internet; instead, they would exist solely for isolated network usage. This certainly reduces risk, but is an expensive and cumbersome alternative. The advice here is that for critical systems, especially those involving safety and life-critical applications, if such segregation is feasible then it is probably worth the additional expense. In any event, additional research in multimode systems that ensure avoidance of dual-homing between networks is imperative and recommended for national infrastructure protection.

> Dual-homing creates another area of vulnerability for enterprise networks.

> Imposing strict policies regarding connection of laptops, PCs, and mobile devices to a network is both cumbersome and expensive but necessary.

Insider Separation

The insider threat in national infrastructure protection is especially tough to address because it is relatively easy for determined adversaries to obtain trusted positions in groups with responsibility for national assets. This threat has become even more difficult to counter as companies continue to partner, purchase, and outsource across political boundaries. Thus, the ease with which an adversary in one country can gain access to the internal, trusted infrastructure systems of another country is both growing and troubling.

> An adversarial threat may come from a trusted partner.

Traditionally, governments have dealt with this challenge through strict requirements on background checking of any individuals who require access to sensitive government systems. This practice continues in many government procurement settings, especially ones involving military or intelligence information. The problem is that national infrastructure includes so much more than just sensitive government systems. It includes SCADA systems, telecommunications networks, transportation infrastructure, financial networks, and the like. Rarely, if ever, are requirements embedded in these commercial environments to ensure some sort of insider controls against unauthorized data collection, inappropriate access to customer records, or administrative access to critical applications. Instead, it is typical for employees to be granted access to the corporate Intranet, from which virtually anything can be obtained.

> The commercially run components of our national infrastructure do not have the same stringent personnel requirements as the government-run components.

Techniques for reducing the risk of unauthorized insider access do exist that can be embedded in the design and operation of national infrastructure operation. These techniques include the following:

- *Internal firewalls*—Internal firewalls separating components of national assets can reduce the risk of insider access. Insiders with access to component A, for example, would have to successfully negotiate through a firewall to gain access to component B. Almost every method for separating insiders from assets will include some sort of internal firewall. They can be implemented as fully configured firewalls, or as packet filtering routers; but regardless, the method of separating insiders from assets using firewalls must become a pervasive control in national infrastructure.

- *Deceptive honey pots*—As we discussed in Chapter 2, internal honey pots can help identify malicious insiders. If the deception is openly advertised, then malicious insiders might be more uncertain in their sabotage activity; if the deception is stealth, however, then operators might observe malicious behavior and potentially identify the internal source.

- *Enforcement of data markings*—Many organizations with responsibility for national infrastructure do not properly mark their information. Every company and government agency must identify, define, and enforce clearly visible data markings on all information that could be mishandled. Without such markings, the likelihood of proprietary information being made available inadvertently to adversaries increases substantially. Some companies have recently begun to use new data markings for personally identifiable information (PII).

- *Data leakage protection (DLP) systems*—Techniques for sniffing gateway traffic for sensitive or inappropriate materials are becoming common. Tools called DLP systems are routinely deployed in companies and agencies. At best, they provide weak protection against insider threats, but they do help identify erroneous leaks. Once deployed, they provide statistics on where and how insiders might be using corporate systems to spill information. In practice, however, no knowledgeable insider would ever be caught by a data leakage tool. Instead, the leak would be done using non-company-provided computers and networks.

One of the more effective controls against insider threats involves a procedural practice that can be embedded into virtually every operation of an organization. The technique is known as *segregation of duties*, and it should be familiar to anyone who has dealt with Sarbanes-Oxley requirements in the United States. Security researchers will recognize the related *separation of duties* notion introduced in the Clark-Wilson integrity model. In both cases, critical work functions are decomposed so that work completion requires multiple individuals to be involved. For example, if a financial task requires two different types of activities for completion, then a segregation of duties requirement would ensure that no one individual could ever perform both operations.

> Segregation of duties offers another layer of protection.

The purpose of this should be obvious. By ensuring that multiple individuals are involved in some sensitive or critical task, the possibility of a single insider committing sabotage is greatly reduced. Of course, multiple individuals could still collude to create an internal attack, but this is more difficult and less likely in most cases. If desired, the risk of multiple individuals creating sabotage can be reduced by more complex segregation of duty policies, perhaps supported by the use of security architectural controls, probably based on internally positioned firewalls. In fact, for network-based segregation tasks, the use of internal firewalls is the most straightforward implementation.

> Internal firewalls create a straightforward *de facto* separation of duties.

In general, the concept of segregation of duties can be represented via a work function ABC that is performed either by a single operator A or as a series of work segments by multiple operators. This general schema supports most instances of segregation of duties, regardless of the motivation or implementation details (see Figure 3.9).

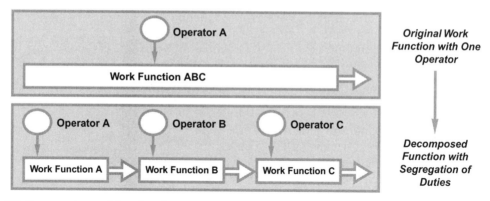

Figure 3.9 Decomposing work functions for segregation of duty.

The idea of breaking down work functions into components is certainly not new. Managers have decomposed functions into smaller tasks for many years; this is how assembly lines originated. Unfortunately, most efforts at work function decomposition result in increased bureaucracy and decreased worker (and end-user) satisfaction. The stereotyped image arises of the government bureau where customers must stand in line at this desk for this function and then stand in line at that desk for that function, and so on. The process is clearly infuriating but, ironically, is also difficult to sabotage by a malicious insider.

The challenge for national infrastructure protection is to integrate segregation of duty policies into all aspects of critical asset management and operation, but to do so in a manner that minimizes the increased bureaucracy. This will be especially difficult in government organizations where the local culture always tends to nurture and embrace new bureaucratic processes.

> How to effectively separate duties without increasing the unwieldy bureaucracy is a challenge that must be addressed.

Asset Separation

Asset separation involves the distribution, replication, decomposition, or segregation of national assets to reduce the risk of an isolated compromise. Each of these separation techniques can be described as follows:

- *Distribution* involves creating functionality using multiple cooperating components that work together as a distributed system. The security advantage is that if the distributed system is designed properly then one or more of the components can be compromised without breaking the overall system function.
- *Replication* involves copying assets across disparate components so that if one asset is broken then replicated versions

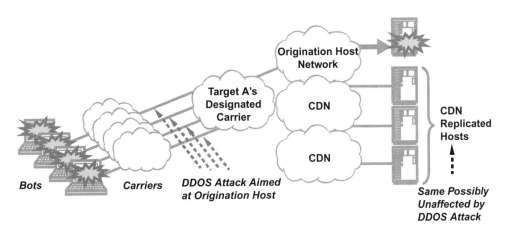

Figure 3.10 Reducing DDOS risk through CDN-hosted content.

will continue to be available. Database systems have been protected in this way for many years. Obviously, no national asset should exist without a degree of replication to reduce risk.

- *Decomposition* is the breaking down of complex assets into individual components so that isolated compromise of a component will be less likely to break the overall asset. A common implementation of a complex business process, for example, generally includes some degree of decomposition into smaller parts.
- *Segregation* is the logical separation of assets through special access controls, data markings, and policy enforcement. Operating systems, unfortunately, provide weak controls in this regard, largely because of the massive deployment of single-user machines over the past couple of decades. Organizations thus implement logical separation of data by trying to keep it on different PCs and laptops. This is a weak implementation.

Each of these techniques is common in modern infrastructure management. For example, content distribution networks (CDNs) are rarely cited as having a positive impact on national infrastructure security, but the reality is that the distribution and replication inherent in CDNs for hosting are powerful techniques for reducing risk. DDOS attacks, for example, are more difficult to complete against CDN-hosted content than for content resident only on an origination host. Attackers have a more difficult time targeting a single point of failure in a CDN (see Figure 3.10).

It is important to emphasize that the use of a CDN certainly does not ensure protection against a DDOS attack, but the replication and distribution inherent in a CDN will make the attack more difficult. By having the domain name system (DNS) point

> Segregation is one method of separation.

to CDN-distributed assets, the content naturally becomes more robust. National infrastructure designers and operators are thus obliged to ensure that CDN hosting is at least considered for all critically important content, especially multimedia content (streaming and progressive download) and any type of critical software download.

This is becoming more important as multimedia provision becomes more commonly embedded into national assets. In the recent past, the idea of providing video over the Internet was nothing more than a trivial curiosity. Obviously, the massive proliferation of video content on sites such as YouTube.com has made these services more mainstream. National assets that rely on video should thus utilize CDN services to increase their robustness. Additional DDOS protection of content from the backbone service provider would also be recommended.

> The increase in multimedia components within national infrastructure networks argues for increased reliance on CDN services.

Multilevel Security (MLS)

A technique for logical separation of assets that was popular in the computer security community during the 1980s and 1990s is known as multilevel security (MLS). MLS operating systems and applications were marketed aggressively to the security community during that time period. A typical implementation involved embedding mandatory access controls and audit trail hooks into the underlying operating system kernel. Assurance methods would then be used to ensure that the trusted component of the kernel was correct, or at least as correct as could be reasonably verified. Today, for reasons largely economic, MLS systems are no longer available, except in the most esoteric classified government applications.

> The familiar notion of "top-secret clearance" comes from MLS systems.

The idea behind MLS was that, by labeling the files and directories of a computer system with meaningful classifications and by also labeling the users of that system with meaningful clearances, a familiar security policy could be enforced. This scheme, which was motivated largely by paper methods used to protect information in government, produced a logical separation of certain assets from certain users, based on the existing policy. For example, files marked "secret" could only be read by users with sufficient clearances. Similarly, users not cleared to the level of "top secret" would not be allowed to read files that were so labeled. The result was an enforced policy on requesting users and protected assets (see Figure 3.11).

Several models of computer system behavior with such MLS functionality were developed in the early years of computer

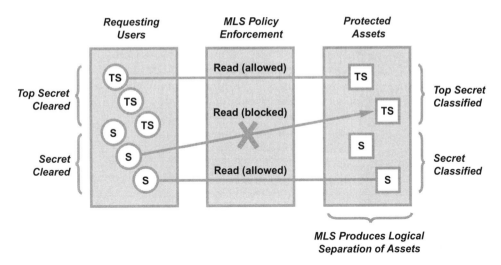

Figure 3.11 Using MLS logical separation to protect assets.

security. The Bell-La Padula disclosure and Biba integrity models
are prominent examples. Each of these models stipulated policy
rules that, if followed, would help to ensure certain desirable
security properties. Certainly, there were problems, especially as
networking was added to isolated secure systems, but, unfortunately, most research and development in MLS dissolved myste-
riously in the mid-1990s, perhaps as a result of the economic pull
of the World Wide Web. This is unfortunate, because the functionality inherent in such MLS separation models would be valuable
in today's national infrastructure landscape. A renewed interest
in MLS systems is thus strongly encouraged to improve protection of any nation's assets.

> MLS systems seem to have
> gone by the wayside
> but should be revived as
> another weapon in the
> national infrastructure
> protection arsenal.

Implementing a National Separation Program

Implementation of a national separation program would involve verification and validation of certain design goals
in government agencies and companies with responsibility for national infrastructure. These goals, related to policy
enforcement between requesting users and the protected national assets, would include the following:

- *Internet separation*—Certain critical national assets simply should not be accessible from the Internet. One would
  imagine that the control systems for a nuclear power plant, for example, would be good candidates for separation
  from the Internet. Formal national programs validating such separation would be a good idea. If this requires changes
  in business practice, then assistance and guidance would be required to transition from open, Internet connectivity
  to something more private.
- *Network-based firewalls*—National infrastructure systems should be encouraged to utilize network-based firewalls,
  preferably ones managed by a centralized group. The likelihood is higher in such settings that signatures will be

kept up to date and that security systems will be operated properly on a 24/7 basis. Procurement programs in government, in particular, must begin to routinely include the use of network-based security in any contract with an Internet service provider.

- *DDOS protection*—All networks associated with national assets should have a form of DDOS protection arranged before an attack occurs. This protection should be provided on a high-capacity backbone that will raise the bar for attackers contemplating a capacity-based cyber attack. If some organization, such as a government agency, does not have a suitable DDOS protection scheme, this should be likened to having no disaster recovery program.

- *Internal separation*—Critical national infrastructure settings must have some sort of incentive to implement an internal separation policy to prevent sabotage. The Sarbanes-Oxley requirements in the United States attempted to enforce such separation for financial systems. While the debate continues about whether this was a successful initiative, some sort of program for national infrastructure seems worth considering. Validation would be required that internal firewalls exist to create protection domains around critical assets.

- *Tailoring requirements*—Incentives must be put in place for vendors to consider building tailored systems such as firewalls for specialized SCADA environments. This would greatly reduce the need for security administrators in such settings to configure their networks in an open position.

Obviously, once a national program is in place, consideration of how one might separate assets between different cooperating nations would seem a logical extension. Certainly, this would seem a more distant goal given the complexity and difficulty of creating validated policy enforcement in one nation.

4

DIVERSITY

We are looking at computers the way a physician would look at genetically related patients, each susceptible to the same disorder.
Mike Reiter, professor of electrical and computer engineering and computer science at Carnegie-Mellon University[1]

Making national infrastructure more diverse in order to create greater resilience against cyber attack seems to be a pretty sensible approach. For example, natural scientists have known for years that a diverse ecosystem is always more resilient to disease than a monoculture. When a forest includes only one tree, the possibility arises that a single disease could wipe out the entire ecosystem. This type of situation arises even in business. Certain airlines, for example, have decided to use only one model of aircraft. This reduces the cost of maintenance and training but does create a serious risk if that particular aircraft were grounded for some reason. The airline would be out of business—a risk that is avoided by a diversity approach.

So it would stand to reason that the process of securing any set of national assets should always include some sort of diversity strategy. This diversity should extend to all applications, software, computers, networks, and systems. Unfortunately, with the exception of familiar geographic requirements on network routes and data centers, diversity is not generally included in infrastructure protection. In fact, the topic of deliberately introducing diversity into national infrastructure to increase its security has not been well explored by computer scientists. Only recently have some researchers begun to investigate the benefits of diversity in software deployment.

> Introducing diversity at all levels of functionality has not been properly explored as a protection strategy.

Diversity in national infrastructure involves the introduction of intentional *differences* into systems. Relevant differences include the vendor source, deployment approach, network connectivity, targeted standards, programming language, operating

---

[1] Quoted in "Taking Cues from Mother Nature to Foil Cyber Attacks" (press release), Office of Legislative and Public Affairs, National Science Foundation, Washington, D.C., 2003 (http://www.nsf.gov/od/lpa/news/03/pr03130.htm).

Cyber Attacks. DOI: 10.1016/B978-0-12-384917-5.00004-4

System	Vendor Source	Deployment Approach	Network Connectivity	Targeted Standards	Programming Language	Operating System	
							◄ - - *Attributes*
A	Company X	Off-the-shelf	IP	IP sec	C++	Windows	◄ - - *A and B:*
B	Company Y	Custom	TDM	None	Java	Unix	◄ - *Diverse*
C	Company Z	Custom	TDM	None	Java	Unix	◄ - - *B and C:* ◄ - - *Non diverse*

Figure 4.1 Diverse and nondiverse components through attribute differences.

system, application base, software version, and so on. Two systems are considered diverse if their key attributes differ, and nondiverse otherwise (see Figure 4.1).

The general idea is that an adversary will make assumptions about each of the relevant attributes in a target system. In the absence of diversity, a worst-case scenario results if the adversary makes the right assumptions about each attribute. If, for example, the adversary creates an attack on a set of computers that assumes an underlying Microsoft® operating system environment, and the national asset at risk employs only these types of systems, then the effect could be significant. In the presence of diversity, however, it becomes much more difficult for an adversary to create an attack with maximal reach. This is especially relevant for attacks that are designed to automatically propagate. Eventually, the attack will reach a point where it can no longer copy itself or remotely execute, and the process will cease.

> Diversity increases the number of assumptions an adversary has to make about the system and creates more potential for an adversary's plan to fail.

Why, then, is diversity so underrepresented in national infrastructure protection? To understand this, one must first recognize the near-obsessive goal of enforcing sets of common standards that the information technology and security communities have attempted to achieve. In nearly every facet of computing, sets of standard, auditable practices have been defined and backed by powerful organizations. In the United States, the Sarbanes-Oxley standard has had a profound influence on the operation of every major corporation in the country, leading to more common approaches to financial systems operation. Commonality, as we discuss in the next chapter, is somewhat at odds with diversity.

> Standardized operations are important for compliance but are at odds with diversity.

This focus on maintaining common, standard operating environments should not come as a surprise. The rise of the Internet, for example, was driven largely by the common acceptance of a single protocol suite. Even the provision of Internet-based services such as websites and mail servers requires agreement among system administrators to follow common port assignments. Chaos would ensue if every administrator decided to assign random ports to their Internet services; end users would not be able to easily locate what they need, and the Internet would be a mess (although this would certainly complicate broad types of attacks). So, the result is general agreement on common computing configurations.

Another key motivation to avoid diversity for most system managers is the costs involved. Typical computing and net-working management teams have created programs focused on removing differences in enterprise systems in order to reduce operating expenses. Clearly, nondiverse information technology systems simplify platform deployment, end-user training, system administrative practices, and system documentation. For these cost-related reasons, diversity is generally not a prominent goal in most current national infrastructure settings. The result is less secure infrastructure.

> Diversity currently competes with commonality and cost savings.

Diversity and Worm Propagation

The self-propagation of a computer worm is a good example of an attack that relies on a nondiverse target environment to function properly. The box shows how relatively simple an attack can be.

Worm Functionality in Three Easy Steps

The functionality of a typical, generic computer worm is quite straightforward (only three steps) and can be described in simple pseudo-code terms as follows:

Program: *Worm*
Start
    Step 1. Find a target system on the network for propagation of Program *Worm*.
    Step 2. Copy Program *Worm* to that target system.
    Step 3. Remotely execute Program *Worm* on that target system.
Repeat Steps 1 through 3.

As you can see, a worm program relies on the ability to find common, reachable, interoperable systems on the network that will accept and execute a copy of the worm program. In the early days of the Internet, this would be accomplished by checking a local file that would include a list of systems that were reachable. Today, it's done by creating batches of Internet Protocol

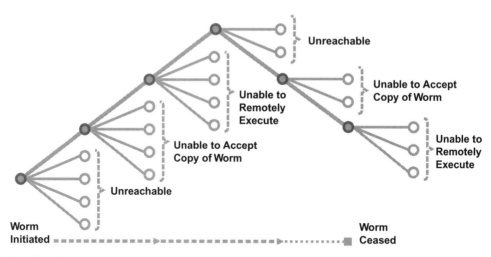

Figure 4.2 Mitigating worm activity through diversity.

A worm propagates by finding interoperable systems to target.

addresses. Also, in those early days, it was quite easy to copy and execute programs from one system to another, because no one had yet invented the firewall.

One would have hoped that the global deployment of firewalls would have stopped the ability of adversaries to create worms, but sadly it has not. Instead, vulnerabilities or services open through the firewalls are used as the basis for worms. Nondiversity in such setups is also the norm. This is unfortunate, because if a worm operates in a diverse environment, and thus cannot find systems that consistently meet one or more of these criteria, then its propagation will cease more rapidly. This can be depicted in a simple reachability diagram showing the point of initiation for the worm through its propagation to the final point at which the activity ceases as a result of diversity. As the worm tries to propagate, diversity attributes that reduce its ability to locate reachable systems, make copies, and remotely execute are the most effective (see Figure 4.2).

Obviously, all worms will eventually cease to propagate, regardless of the degree of diversity in a given network. The security advantage one gains with diversity is that the worm is likely to cease more quickly and perhaps without human intervention. Empirical experience in the global security community dealing with worms such as the SQL/Slammer and Blaster worms of 2003 and the Sasser worm of 2004 suggest that significant human intervention is required to halt malicious operation. During the early hours of the SQL/Slammer worm, most of the security incident response calls involved people trying to figure out what to do. Eventually, the most effective solution involved putting local area network blocks in place to shut down the offending traffic. By the time the event died down, many millions of hours of global labor had been expended working on the problem. By increasing diversity, one should expect to reduce response costs around the world associated with fighting worms.

The real challenge here is that both the Internet and the networks and systems being run by companies and agencies charged with national infrastructure are simply not diverse—and there is little discussion in place to alter this situation. As we suggested earlier, this is driven largely by the goal to maximize interoperability. There are some exceptions in the broader computing community, such as digital rights management (DRM)-based systems that have tended to limit the execution of certain content applications to very specific devices such as the iPod® and iPhone®. The general trend, however, is toward more open, interoperable computing. What this means is that, for national infrastructure components that must be resilient against automated attacks such as worms, the threat will remain as long as the networking environment is a monoculture.

> Although introducing security can seem expensive, one should expect to save money on response costs with an effective diverse environment.

Desktop Computer System Diversity

Typical individual computer users in the home or office, regardless of their location in the world, are most likely to be using a commercial operating system running on a standard processor platform and utilizing one of a couple of popular browsers to perform searches on a popular search engine. This might seem an obvious statement, but in the early days of computing there were many users on home-grown or proprietary systems using all sorts of software that might only be known locally.

Today, however, the most likely configuration would be a Windows®-based operating system on an Intel® platform with Internet Explorer® being used for Google® searches. We can say this confidently, because almost all current estimates of market share list these products as dominant in their respective fields. Certainly, competing platforms and services from Apple® and others have made inroads, but for the most part, especially in business and government environments, the desktop configuration is highly predictable (see Figure 4.3).

> The average home PC user is working in a highly predictable computing environment.

This dominant position for these few companies has admittedly led to a number of positive results. It has, for instance, pushed a deeper common understanding of computing among individuals around the world. Different people from different

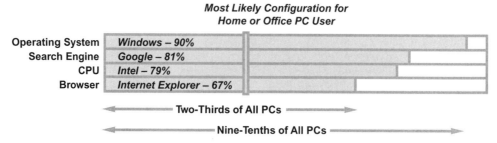

Figure 4.3 Typical PC configuration showing nondiversity.

cultures around the world can share their experiences, recommendations, and suggestions about operating systems, search engines, CPUs, and browsers, and the likelihood of applicability is high. The dominant position of these respective products has also helped the software development industry by creating rich and attractive common target markets. Developers generally love to see a dominant platform configuration, because it increases their potential profits through maximal usage. So, computing certainly has moved forward as a result of commonality; not much disagreement exists on this point.

The drawback from a national infrastructure perspective, however, is that adversaries will have an easier time creating attacks with significant reach and implication. Just as a game of dominoes works best when each domino is uniformly designed and positioned, so does common infrastructure become easier to topple with a single, uniform push. In some cases, the effect is significant; the operating system market on desktop PCs, for example, is dominated by Microsoft® to the point where a well-designed Windows®-based attack could be applicable to 90% of its desktop targets.

> Targeting the most popular operating system software with a worm attack could bring the majority of PCs to a standstill.

More likely, however, is the situation where the creation of a botnet becomes much easier given the nondiversity of PC configurations. When a botnet operator conceptualizes the design of a new botnet, the most important design consideration involves reach. That is, the botnet operator will seek to create malware that has the maximal likelihood of successfully infecting the largest number of target PCs. As such, the nondiversity of end-user configurations plays right into the hands of the botnet operator. Combine this with the typically poor system administrative practices on most PCs, and the result is lethal. Worse, many security managers in business and government do not understand this risk. When trying to characterize the risk of attack, they rarely understand that the problem stems from a global set of nondiverse end-user PCs being mismanaged by home and office workers.

> Security managers are unlikely to consider the home PC user when assessing risk.

In response to this threat, national infrastructure protection requires a deliberate and coordinated introduction of diversity into the global desktop computing environment. Enterprise attention is obviously different than that of individuals in homes, but the same principle applies. If the desktop computing assets that can reach a national asset must be maximally resilient, then desktop diversity is worth considering. The most obvious challenge here is related to the consumer marketplace for PCs; that is, the reason why consumers use the same platform is because they prefer it and have chosen to purchase it. If Microsoft® and Intel®, for example, were not providing value in their products, then people would buy something else. The biggest hurdle, therefore, involves enabling nondiversity without altering the ability of companies to provide products that people like to use. Perhaps this goal could be accomplished via diversity elements coming from within the existing vendor base.

Desktop Diversity Considerations

Additional issues that arise immediately with respect to desktop diversity programs include the following:

- *Platform costs*—By introducing multiple, diverse platforms into a computing environment, the associated hardware and software costs might increase. This is a common justification by information technology (IT) managers for avoiding diversity initiatives. Certainly, the procurement of larger volumes of a given product will reduce the unit cost, but by introducing competition into the PC procurement arena increased costs might be somewhat mitigated.
- *Application interoperability*—Multiple, diverse platforms will complicate organizational goals to ensure common interoperability of key applications across all platforms. This can be managed by trying to match the desktop platform to local needs, but the process is not trivial. The good news is that most web-based applications behave similarly on diverse platforms.
- *Support and training*—Multiple, diverse platforms will complicate support and training processes by adding a new set of vendor concerns. In practical terms, this often means introducing a platform such as Mac OS® to a more traditional Windows®-based environment. Because many consumers are comfortable with both platforms, especially youngsters who tend to be more diverse in their selections, the problem is not as intense as it might be.

For national infrastructure protection, desktop diversity initiatives that are focused on ensuring enterprise differences in companies and agencies have a good chance of success. Rewards and incentives can be put in place to mix up the desktop platforms in a given enterprise. The problem is that this will have only limited usefulness from the perspective of botnet design and recruitment. The real advantage would come from diversity in

> Global diversity in broadband-connected home PCs would stymie many botnet attacks.

broadband-connected PCs run by consumers around the world. Unfortunately, this is not something that can be easily controlled via an initiative in any country, including the United States.

Interestingly, a related problem that emerges is the seemingly widespread software piracy one finds in certain areas of the globe. Software piracy on the desktop introduces the problem of security updates; that is, depending on the specifics of the theft, it is often difficult for pirated PCs to be properly protected with required patches. When many millions of PCs are in this state, the problem of nondiversity becomes all the more severe.

Diversity Paradox of Cloud Computing

To better understand how diversity goals can be accomplished, it helps to introduce a simple model of desktop computing systems. The model is represented as a linear spectrum of options related to the degree to which systems are either diverse or nondiverse. As such, the two ends of the model spectrum are easy to identify for a given environment. On one side of the spectrum would be the option of complete nondiversity, where every desktop system in the organization, enterprise, or group is exactly the same. On the other side of the spectrum would be the option of complete diversity across the organization, where no two desktop systems are the same. In the middle of the spectrum would be the usual types of settings, where some minor degree of diversity exists, but with a clearly dominant platform.

The model spectrum is useful because it allows illustration of our basic infrastructure security proposition around PCs—namely, as diversity increases, desktop attacks, including the use of worms to create a local denial of service condition, are more difficult to accomplish. One might also suggest that the creation and use of botnets would also be more difficult, but this benefit might be more modest (see Figure 4.4).

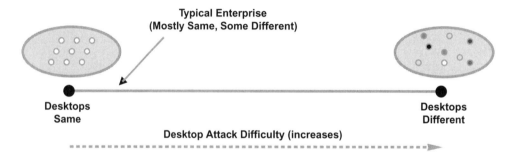

Figure 4.4 Spectrum of desktop diversity options.

In fact, diverse desktops are tougher to uniformly compromise, because they are less conducive as a group to a scalable, self-propagating attack. For example, if a company has half of its PCs running Windows®-based operating systems and half running Mac OS®-based operating systems, then this will clearly be more challenging for an automatically propagating attack. Hence, the level of diversity and the associated difficulty of attack appear to correlate. A challenge with this view, however, is that it does not properly characterize the optimal choice in reducing desktop attack risk—namely, the *removal* of desktops from the target environment. After all, one cannot attack systems that are not even there. This suggests a new (and admittedly theoretical) diversity and attack difficulty spectrum (see Figure 4.5).

> As the level of diversity increases, the level of difficulty for an attack likewise increases.

This suggests that the ultimate (albeit impossible) option for making desktops more secure involves their removal. Obviously, this is not a practical goal, but computer security objectives are often made more tractable via clear statements of the ideal condition. So, while current enterprise or home computing architectures do not include the option of having no desktop computers, older readers will remember the days when desktops did not exist. Rather, people used computer terminals to access information on mainframes, and security benefits were certainly present in such a setup. This included no need for end-user software patching, as well as no end-user platform for targeted malware. One great irony in the present deployment of desktops to every man, woman, and child on the planet is that most people really do not need such computing power. It is likely that they would be just fine with a keyboard, screen, and mouse connected to network-resident applications that are ubiquitously available via the Internet.

> The global proliferation of home PCs has increased the risk of malware attacks.

In modern computing, the closest thing we have to this arrangement is virtualized, cloud-based computing. In such a setup, computing power and application intelligence move to a centralized complex of servers, accessible via light clients. In

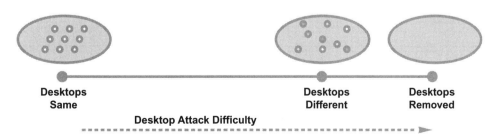

Figure 4.5 Diversity and attack difficulty with option of removal.

fact, handheld mobile devices provide the equivalent of a desktop computer in such a cloud environment. One should therefore presume, from the diagram in Figure 4.5, that cloud computing would provide considerable security benefits by removing non-diverse desktops from the environment. This is most likely true, as long as the infrastructure supporting the cloud applications is properly secured, as per the various principles described in this book. If this is not the case, then one is simply moving nondiversity vulnerabilities from the desktops to the servers.

> Cloud computing may offer home PC users the diverse, protected environment they cannot otherwise access.

Network Technology Diversity

Modern telecommunications network systems can be viewed as consisting of the following two basic types of technologies:

- *Circuit-switched*—This includes legacy, circuit-switched systems that support traditional plain old telephone services (POTS) and related voice and data services. The public switched telephone network (PSTN) is the most significant example of deployed circuit-switched technology.
- *Packet-switched*—This includes more modern, packet-switched systems that support Internet Protocol (IP) and related voice, data, and multimedia services. In addition to the Internet as the most obvious example of packet switching, the signaling network controlling the PSTN is itself a packet-switched system.

For the most part, both logical and physical diversity naturally exist between these two types of services, largely due to technology interoperability. That is, the vast majority of equipment, software, processes, and related infrastructure for these services are fundamentally different. Packets cannot accidentally or intentionally spill into circuits, and *vice versa*.

> Circuit-switched and packet-switched systems automatically provide diversity when compared to one another.

From a networking perspective, what this means is that a security event that occurs in one of these technologies will generally not have any effect on the other. For example, if a network worm is unleashed across the Internet, as the global community experienced so severely in the 2003–2004 time frame, then the likelihood that this would affect traditional time-division multiplexed (TDM) voice and data services is negligible. Such diversity is of significant use in protecting national infrastructure, because it becomes so much more difficult for a given attack such as a worm to scale across logically separate technologies (see Figure 4.6).

Even with the logical diversity inherent in these different technologies, one must be careful in drawing conclusions. A more

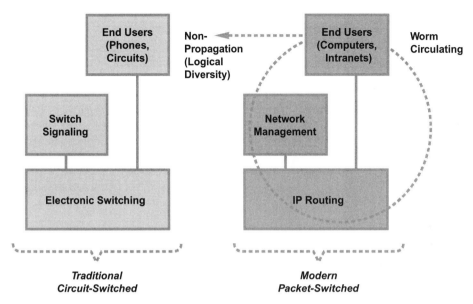

Figure 4.6 Worm nonpropagation benefit from diverse telecommunications.

accurate view of diverse telecommunications, for example, might expose the fact that, at lower levels, shared transport infrastructure might be present. For example, many telecommunications companies use the same fiber for their circuit-switched delivery as they do for IP-based services. Furthermore, different carriers often use the same right-of-way for their respective fiber delivery. What this means is that in many locations such as bridges, tunnels, and major highways, a physical disaster or targeted terrorist attack could affect networks that were designed to be carrier diverse.

> Unfortunately, vulnerabilities will always be present in IP-based and circuit-switched systems.

While sharing of fiber and right-of-way routes makes sense from an operational implementation and cost perspective, one must be cognizant of the shared infrastructure, because it does change the diversity profile. As suggested, it complicates any reliance on a multivendor strategy for diversity, but it also makes it theoretically possible for an IP-based attack, such as one producing a distributed denial of service (DDOS) effect, that would have negative implications on non-IP-based transport due to volume. This has not happened in practical settings to date, but because so much fiber is shared it is certainly a possibility that must be considered (see Figure 4.7).

A more likely scenario is that a given national service technology, such as modern 2G and 3G wireless services for citizens

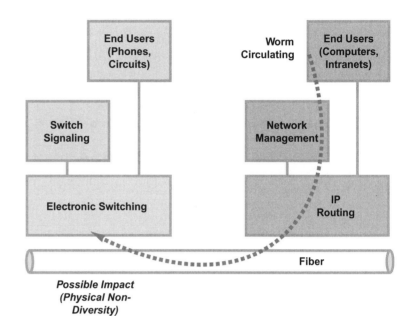

Figure 4.7 Potential for impact propagation over shared fiber.

and business, could see security problems stemming from either circuit- or packet-switched-based attacks. Because a typical carrier wireless infrastructure, for example, will include both a circuit- and packet-switched core, attacks in either area could cause problems. Internet browsing and multimedia messaging could be hit by attacks at the serving and gateway systems for these types of services; similarly, voice services could be hit by attacks on the mobile switching centers supporting this functionality. So, while it might be a goal to ensure some degree of diversity in these technology dependencies, in practice this may not be possible.

Diversity may not always be a feasible goal.

What this means from a national infrastructure protection perspective is that maximizing diversity will help to throttle large-scale attacks, but one must be certain to look closely at the entire architecture. In many cases, deeper inspection will reveal that infrastructure advertised as diverse might actually have components that are not. This does not imply that sufficient mitigations are always missing in nondiverse infrastructure, but rather that designers must take the time to check. When done properly, however, network technology diversity remains an excellent means for reducing risk. Many a security officer will report, for example, the comfort of knowing that circuit-switched voice services will generally survive worms, botnets, and viruses on the Internet.

Physical Diversity

The requirement for physical diversity in the design of computing infrastructure is perhaps the most familiar of all diversity-related issues. The idea is that any computing or networking asset that serves as an essential component of some critical function must include physical distribution to increase its survivability. The approach originated in the disaster recovery community with primary emphasis on natural disasters such as hurricanes and fires, but, as the security threat has matured, infrastructure managers have come to recognize the value of providing some degree of physical diversity. This reduces, for example, reliance on a single local power grid, which is a valued cyber attack target for adversaries. It also greatly reduces the chances of a physical or premise-based attack, simply because multiple facilities would be involved.

> Physical diversity adds another important layer of protection against cascading effects.

These issues are not controversial. In fact, for many years, procurement projects for national asset systems, in both government and industry, have routinely included the demand that the following physical diversity issues be considered:

- *Backup center diversity*—If any major center for system, network, or application management is included in a given infrastructure component, then it is routinely required that a backup center be identified in a physically diverse location. Few would argue with this approach; if properly applied, it would ensure that the two centers are in different weather patterns and power grid segments.

> Physical diversity has been incorporated into the national asset system for many years.

- *Supplier/vendor diversity*—Many organizations dictate that for critical infrastructure components, some degree of diversity must be present in the supplier and vendor mix. This reduces the likelihood that any given firm would have too much influence on the integrity of the infrastructure. It also reduces the likelihood of a cascading problem that might link back to some common element, such as a software routine or library, embedded in one vendor's product portfolio.
- *Network route diversity*—When network infrastructure is put in place to support national infrastructure, it is not uncommon to demand a degree of network route diversity from the provider or providers. This helps reduce the likelihood of malicious (or nonmalicious) problems affecting connectivity. As mentioned above, this is complicated by common use of bridges, tunnels, or highways for physical network media deployments from several different vendors.

Achieving Physical Diversity via Satellite Data Services

A good example application that demonstrates physical diversity principles is the provision of certain types of SCADA systems using IP over satellite (IPoS). Satellite data services have traditionally had the great advantage of being able to operate robustly via the airwaves in regions around the globe where terrestrial network construction would be difficult. Generally, in such regions commercial wireless coverage is less ubiquitous or even completely unavailable. Some SCADA applications have thus taken advantage of this robust communication feature in satellite systems to connect remote end-user terminals to the SCADA host system, but the requirement remains that some degree of diversity be utilized. As suggested above, most of this diversity emphasis has been driven largely by concerns over natural and physical disasters, but a clear cyber security benefit exists as well.

Generally, the setup for satellite-connected SCADA involves end users connecting to a collection of physically diverse hubs via IPoS. These diverse hubs are then connected in a distributed manner to the SCADA hosts. An adversary seeking to attack these hubs would have to use either logical or electronic means, and a great degree of logistic effort would be required, especially if the hubs are located in different parts of the world. The Hughes Corporation, as an example, has been aggressive in marketing these types of configurations for SCADA customers. Their recommended remote access configuration for diverse SCADA system control is shown in Figure 4.8.

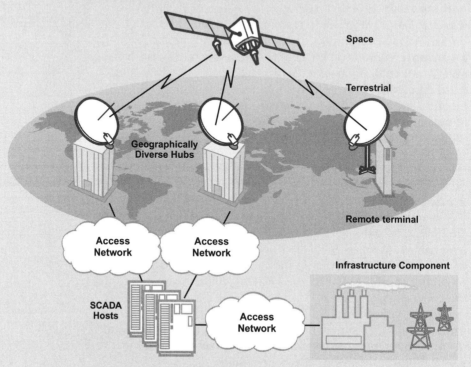

Figure 4.8 Diverse hubs in satellite SCADA configurations.

- *ISO/IEC 27000 Standard (ISO27K)*—The International Organization for Standardization (ISO) and International Electrotechnical Commission (IEC) evolved a British Security Standard known as BS-7799 into an internationally recognized set of auditable security best practices. Some security experts believe that the ISO27K family of security standards is the most global and generally agreed upon set of best practices.

  All of these standards, and the many additional ones that are not mentioned above, include a large subset of security and functional requirements that are virtually the same. For example, each standard requires carefully documented policies and procedures, authentication and authorization controls, data collection systems, and embedded encryption. Each standard also requires management oversight, ongoing security monitoring, compliance scores issued by designated auditors, and some form of fines or punishment if the standard best practices are not met.

With such redundancy in security standards and compliance, one would guess that the principle of commonality would be largely met in national infrastructure protection. For example, some organizations might be required to demonstrate compliance to dozens of different security standards. One would expect that such intense and focused attention on security would lead to a largely common approach to security around the globe. Sadly, the belief here is that in spite of the considerable audit and compliance activity around the world, most of it does not address the type of security commonality that will make a positive difference in national infrastructure protection. The activity instead tends to focus on requirements that have some value but do not address the most critical issues. In fact, most of these practices exist in the category of state-of-the-art security, far beyond the minimally acceptable levels addressed in most audits.

The audit problem stems from the inherent differences between *meaningful* and *measurable* security best practices. There's an old dumb joke about a man looking for his lost money on 42nd and Eighth. When a passerby asks whether the money was actually lost at that spot, the man looks up and says that the money was actually lost over on 41st and Tenth but the light is much better here. Security audit of best practices is often like this; the only practices that can be audited are ones where the light is good and measurable metrics can be established. This does not, however, imply that such metrics are always meaningful (see Figure 5.2).

The example requirements shown in Figure 5.2 provide a hint as to the types of requirements that are likely to be included in each category. One can easily levy a measurable requirement on password length, for example, even though this is generally a less useful constraint. This could be viewed as an example that

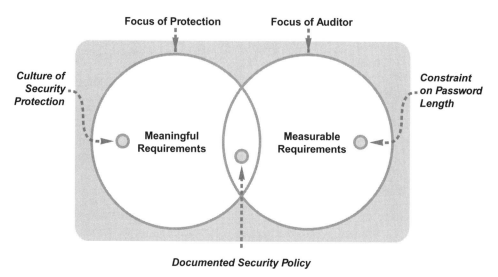

Focus of Protection   Focus of Auditor

Culture of Security Protection

Constraint on Password Length

Meaningful Requirements   **Measurable Requirements**

Documented Security Policy

Figure 5.2 Relationship between meaningful and measurable requirements.

is measurable but not meaningful. Conversely, one can levy the important requirement that a strong culture of security be present in an environment. This is a meaningful condition but almost impossible to measure. The example requirement that a security policy be present is both meaningful and measurable. It demonstrates that there are certainly some requirements that reside in both categories.

> Ideally, security practices are both meaningful *and* measurable.

Meaningful Best Practices for Infrastructure Protection

A provocative implication here is that the ability to audit a given best practice does not determine or influence whether it is useful for infrastructure protection. In fact, the primary motivation for proper infrastructure protection should not be one's audit score; rather, the motivation should be success based and economic. The fact is that companies, agencies, and groups with responsibility for infrastructure protection will eventually fail if they do not follow the best available recommendations for security best practices. Unfortunately, the best recommendations come not from the security standards and audit community but from practical experience.

> A great audit score does not necessarily guarantee successful infrastructure protection.

If you do not agree, then please consider that security standards backed by powerful and authoritative groups have existed for many decades. In addition, security auditors have been in business for decades, performing diligent analysis and issuing embarrassing failure grades to security teams around the world. Our earlier reference to FISMA, for example, included failing grades for many prominent government agencies in the United States. In spite of all this activity and reporting, however, nothing truly material has changed during these past decades in the way computer and network systems are secured. In fact, one could easily make the claim that national infrastructure is more vulnerable to attack today than it was 20 years ago. What makes one think that more stringent security standards and audit processes are going to change this now?

Based on this author's experiences managing the security of major critical infrastructure components for many years, the answer lies in a two-step methodology:

- *Step 1. Standard audit*—The first step is conventional, in that it recommends that every organization submit to a standard audit to ensure that no group is operating below the minimally acceptable threshold. While most organizations would claim to already have this step ongoing, the goal here is to be given a desirable rating or score, rather than a failing one. So, even if a company or agency has ongoing audits, the goal here is to *pass* these audits. Any one of the major audit standards mentioned above is probably acceptable; they all roughly direct the same sort of minimal practices.

> A successful protection strategy should start with at least a passing score on a standard security audit.

- *Step 2. World-class focus*—The second step involves a more intense focus on a set of truly meaningful national infrastructure protection practices. These practices are derived largely from experience. They are consistent with the material presented in this book, and they will only be present in pieces in most existing security audit standards. The greatest success will typically come from organizations self-administering this new focus, especially because these practices are not easy to measure and audit (see Figure 5.3).

For the first step, an important issue involves ensuring that the audit does not cause more harm than good. For example, suppose that a competent and trustworthy system administrator has been charged with a bevy of responsibilities for an infrastructure component and that she has demonstrated excellent results over a long period of time, with no security problems. This is a common situation, especially in companies and agencies that take system administration seriously. Unfortunately, a security auditor would look at such a setup with horror and would deem it a clear violation of least privilege, separation of duties, and so on.

> Sometimes security audit standards and best practices proven through experience are in conflict.

Figure 5.3 Methodology to achieve world-class infrastructure protection practices.

In the United States, if the component being administered was a financial one in a public company, then this would be a violation of the Sarbanes-Oxley segregation of duties requirements. The auditor would typically require that the single competent administrator be replaced by a bureaucratic process involving a team of potentially inferior personnel who would each only see a portion of the total task. It is not difficult to imagine the component being more poorly managed and, hence, less secure. This is the worst case in any audit and must be explicitly avoided for national infrastructure protection.

For the second step, the box lists specific meaningful security best practices, six in total, for national infrastructure protection. These six best practices do not contradict current auditing processes and standards, but they are certainly not designed for easy audit application; for example, it is difficult to validate whether something is "appropriate" or "simplified." Nevertheless, our strong advice is that attentiveness to ensuring commonality across national infrastructure with these six practices will yield significant benefits.

Six Best Practices for National Infrastructure Protection

- *Practice 1. Locally relevant and appropriate security policy*—Every organization charged with the design or operation of national infrastructure must have a security policy that is locally relevant to the environment and appropriate to the organizational mission. This implies that different organizations should expect to have different security policies. The good news is that this policy requirement is largely consistent with most standards and should be one of the more straightforward practices to understand.
- *Practice 2. Organizational culture of security protection*—Organizations charged with national infrastructure must develop and nurture a culture of security protection. The culture must pervade the organization and must include

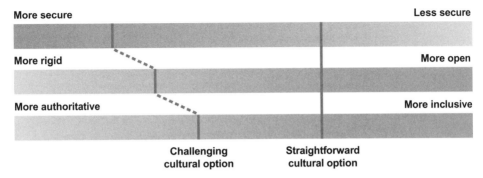

Figure 5.5 Spectrum of organizational culture of security options.

security culture should not be required in all cases, regardless of any cultural goals of being open, creative, and willing to interact publicly. The U.S. military, for example, might exemplify such a level of rigid cultural commitment to security. One answer, as we've discussed above, is that it is difficult to *require* that a culture be in place in an organization. Specific aspects of a culture might be required such as strong policy, tough enforcement, and so on, but to require the presence of a culture is easy to confirm. Nevertheless, the premise is correct; that is, for national infrastructure, certain security standards are required that can only be met in an environment where a culture of security protection is met. This demands the uncomfortable situation in which local managers must honestly work to create the appropriate culture, which in some cases might require decades of attention.

> Implementation of a true culture of security cannot happen overnight; it may take years to develop.

An important element of security culture is the symbolism that management can create by its own behavior. This means that when senior executives are given passes that allow policy violations, this is a serious error as it detracts from the cultural objectives. Unfortunately, the most senior executives almost always outrank security staff, and this practice of senior exemption is all too common. Perhaps major national infrastructure solicitations should include questions about this type of senior executive practice before contracts can be granted to an organization. This might give the security team more concrete ammunition to stop such exemptions.

> A true culture of security must be implemented at all levels of an organization—including the most senior executives.

Infrastructure Simplification

Our third recommended common practice involves an explicit organizational commitment to infrastructure simplification. Defining what we mean by simplification in the context of

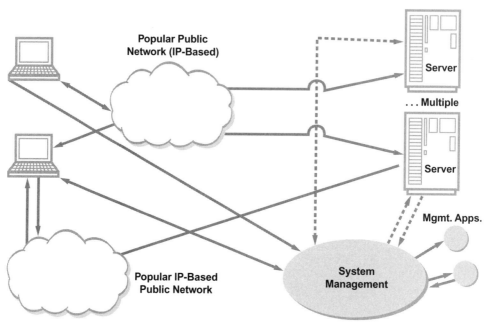

Figure 5.6 Sample cluttered engineering chart.

infrastructure requires that we use subjective language. Simpler infrastructure is easier to understand, less cumbersome, and more streamlined. As such, simplification initiatives will be subjective and much more difficult to measure using some quantitative metric. To illustrate this process of simplification, let's look at a typical sort of cluttered engineering schematic that one might use to describe network infrastructure. The chart shown in Figure 5.6 is derived from the design documentation embedded in an infrastructure project with which this author was recently involved. This diagram suffers from the typical sorts of issues that one finds in the design and operation of national infrastructure:

- *Lack of generalization*—Systems in the diagram are not viewed in a generalized manner. The same thing is shown multiple times in different places in the diagram (e.g., servers), rather than just generalizing one component to depict both.
- *Clouding the obvious*—Interfaces in the diagram are not depicted obviously. Lines are cluttered across the drawing, and simple interfaces are clouded to avoid what is actually quite obvious connectivity.
- *Stream-of-consciousness design*—The diagram seems to be the product of first-draft, stream-of-consciousness thinking rather than a carefully planned layout. Too often, infrastructure is put

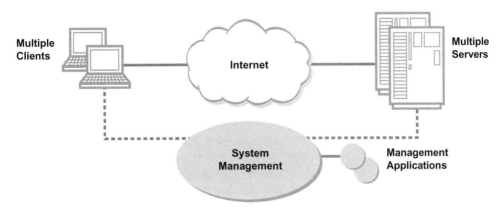

Figure 5.7 Simplified engineering chart.

in place in a first draft without anyone taking the time to review and revise.
- *Nonuniformity*—Objects are not referred to uniformly; the references to an IP-based network are slightly different, and in fact should just reference the Internet anyway.

If one applies some rational simplification to the design in the cluttered chart shown above, with attention to each of the elements just mentioned, then the resultant functionally equivalent product is much easier to understand. The more improved diagram requires that you go back and confirm that it really does describe the same function, but in fact it does (see Figure 5.7).

Analysis of how we simplified the cluttered diagram into something more easily understood highlights some of the techniques that can be useful in simplifying a national infrastructure component environment (see box).

How to Simplify a National Infrastructure (or Otherwise Complex) Environment

- *Reduction in size*—The second diagram is smaller than the first one. Relevance of such action to national infrastructure should be obvious. Simplification should include reduction wherever possible. Less code, fewer interfaces, and reduced functionality are all healthy simplification objectives that will almost certainly improve security. In fact, a requirement for national infrastructure should be demonstrable evidence of software removal or reduction initiatives. The only truly secure piece of code is the one that you have removed.

- *Generalization of concepts*—The second diagram generalizes concepts more effectively than the first. This should be true in national infrastructure as well. Rather than managing dozens or hundreds or thousands of special cases, it is more effective to have a planned generalization strategy that allows for simpler management. Obviously, this requires some balancing with local diversity requirements.
- *Cleaner interfaces*—Perhaps the most obvious difference between the two diagrams is the much cleaner view of interfaces that the second one provides. Because national infrastructure will include complex interfaces between systems, initiatives to simplify these interfaces must be present to optimize security for national assets.
- *Highlighting of patterns*—The second diagram demonstrates functional and data flow patterns in an obvious manner. This simplifies any changes that might have to be made to the architecture. Infrastructure should also be designed in a manner to highlight important patterns in data or processing.
- *Reduction of clutter*—The first diagram is as cluttered as one can imagine, and this generally indicates a stream-of-consciousness design process. Too often, national infrastructure emerges in the same manner, with one system being put in place and then another, they are then connected to something else, and on and on. The result is usually not optimal from a security perspective.

The process of auditing these subjective goals will be challenging, if not intractable, but this does not reduce the importance of trying to attain each goal in national infrastructure. Infrastructure simplification could, in fact, be argued to be the most important single goal in the protection of national assets. One bright spot here is that security managers will find kindred spirits with most information technology managers, although it is the rare CIO who truly knows how to manage the simplification and reduction of infrastructure. A good sign that the local organization is trying would be some sort of initiative focused on the reduction or removal of software applications.

> Simplification may be the first and most tractable step toward creating a new, more secure infrastructure environment.

Certification and Education

Our fourth recommended common practice involves certification and education programs for key decision-makers. Most current computer security education initiatives tend to focus on teaching awareness to end users about proper selection of passwords, storage of data, handing of devices, and so on. These awareness initiatives stem from the common belief that computer and network systems would be perfectly secure if end users would just take the time to learn and follow the security policy rules. The situation is reminiscent of doctors blaming their patients for their diseases.

Security auditors generally agree with this view of end-user responsibility, and they will often perform spot checks in target environments. This usually involves quizzing random individuals about their knowledge and interpretation of the local security policy. When the inevitable bad grade occurs because high percentages of individuals do not know some of the policy rules, security teams are forced to increase the intensity of the awareness program with posters, videos, mandatory tests, and even punishments for end-user ignorance.

Based on decades of experience in performing these types of audits, supporting them, and also being subjected to them, the conclusion reached here is that the goal of reaching 100% end-user awareness of security is impractical. Certainly, security education for end users does not hurt, because everyone should be aware of the risks of any actions they might take that could damage security in the local environment. If end users are entrusted with proprietary information, for example, they need to understand the implications of allowing such information to be provided to unauthorized sources.

> One hundred percent end-user awareness of security policies may remain an illusive goal.

For national infrastructure protection, however, a much more practical goal is to focus primarily on improving the security competence of decision-makers rather than on end users. The distinction here is subtle, but fundamental. Key decision-makers in national infrastructure settings include the following:

- *Senior managers*—These are the people who set financial and operational priorities affecting national infrastructure. They include the most senior managers in an organization or the highest ranking in the military.
- *Designers and developers*—These are the network, system, and application designers and developers who determine what security features and functionality are in the systems that people use. They often work in information technology groups.
- *Administrators*—These are the system and network administrators who perform the day-to-day tasks of maintaining and running the systems that people use. Too often, these folks are underpaid and poorly trained.
- *Security team members*—These are the security staff charged with the organizational systems for protecting assets. An increasing number of organizations outsource aspects of this work. There is nothing wrong with this trend, as long as the arrangement is well managed and coordinated.

These four types of key decision-makers are the people who can make the most substantive difference in the security of an organization and for whom 100% coverage should be a tractable goal. It doesn't hurt that the size of the key decision-maker population in a company or agency will be much smaller than the total population. It also doesn't hurt that they tend to be the

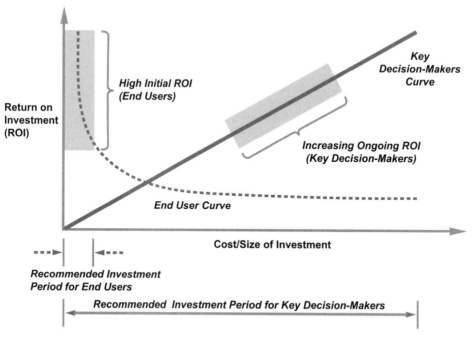

Figure 5.8 Return on investment (ROI) trends for security education.

ones best trained to understand the importance of security. From an investment perspective, the returns on education investment look quite different for end users and decision-makers (see Figure 5.8).

The message embedded in the ROI curves in Figure 5.8 is that a small initial investment in security certification and education for end users produces a reasonable initial return. This return rapidly diminishes, however, because in a typical environment there is only so much an end user can do. In fact, in the best designed environments, the obligation for end users to make security decisions on their own is always minimized. For key decision-makers, the ROI is ongoing and steadily increasing throughout the investment lifecycle. Unlike end users, key decision-makers can consistently apply their increased security knowledge to infrastructure in a meaningful and scalable manner.

To summarize, our recommendation here is a twofold approach for security certification and education in a national infrastructure environment:

- *Key decision-makers*—Focus on providing ongoing, lifecycle programs for decision-makers in security certification and education. By focusing on key decision-makers, the returns will be consistent, increasing, and scalable.

- *End users*—Create low-cost, high-initial-return activities for certifying and educating end users. As a complement, systems must be designed that minimize the decisions end users make about security.

The specific certification and education programs for a given environment should be locally determined and appropriately applied. They are not difficult to find or create but can be misapplied without some careful planning. Well-known security certifications, such as Certified Information Systems Security Professional (CISSP), are excellent for system or network administrators but totally unnecessary for end users. Similarly, awareness programs on selecting good passwords are fine for end users but will just annoy your system administrators.

Career Path and Reward Structure

Our fifth recommended common practice involves the creation and establishment of career paths and reward structures for security professionals. It should come as no surprise that organizations charged with national infrastructure should demonstrate some common form of career path and reward structure for security staff. This is particularly important, because to perform security tasks properly, some degree of longevity is desirable. Too often, important cyber security tasks are attempted by staff who are new to the security discipline and who are poorly compensated for their work.

> Creating career paths and incentives is important in any field, no less so in security management.

Fixing this might seem obvious, but virtually no security standards used for the purposes of audit include this in a meaningful way. Elements that should be commonly present in national infrastructure environments include the following:

- *Attractive salaries*—Infrastructure organizations should demonstrate salary structure that takes into account the specialized skills associated with cyber security. Salaries should be above industry averages, a metric that can be quantitatively audited. (Amazingly, I've never seen security staff salaries audited as part of any due diligence activity by an auditor.)
- *Career paths*—Opportunities for career advancement, promotion, and salary increase should be present in infrastructure organizations. Perhaps more than any other information technology or network-related discipline, security engineering of national infrastructure requires years of experience in order to develop proper judgment. If these years do not include

attention to career issues, then the organization is unlikely to maintain the best staff.

- *Senior managers*—It is desirable for senior managers in infrastructure organizations to have some degree of heritage in the security community. This certainly will help with decision-making at the senior level, but more importantly it serves as a symbol for the security staff that senior level management is attainable from the security ranks.

These career-related organizational attributes are rarely discussed in the context of determining whether proper security is in place in an organization. Auditors never discuss these issues. This is unfortunate, as good salaries and career paths for security staff are more relevant to the overall security posture of an organization than checking for trivia such as password length, timeouts after bad login attempts, and other elements commonly found in security standards.

> A strong indicator of a healthy security environment might be something that is often overlooked, such as heritage of the senior security managers in a company.

It is also worth noting that companies and agencies should not actively recruit and hire individuals who have a history of breaking laws on computers and networks. Hacking, in its original incarnation, was all about the desire to learn and share; when hackers demonstrate this type of perspective, they can easily blend into a company or agency and be productive. The associated career and reward track for such individuals is rarely promotion or money but rather ongoing or increased access to the latest and greatest types of technologies.

Responsible Past Security Practice

Our sixth recommended common practice involves two specific actions: The first is that any company or agency being considered for national infrastructure work should be required to demonstrate past practice in live security incidents. The second is that companies and agencies must do a better job of managing their inventory of live incidents, including databases of key factors, root causes, and security learning from events. These two seemingly obvious actions are almost never performed explicitly, and most companies and agencies do not even maintain formal documentation on past security incidents.

> Companies and agencies should maintain a historical record showing clear incident response documentation.

The good news is that most solicitations for national infrastructure project work do include some requirement for demonstrating past engineering practices, so there is certainly a base on which to improve matters for security. When federal agencies contract for engineering or technical work, for example, boilerplate language is usually embedded into the contract for information on previous projects, similar work activities, and lists of reference clients. This practice is appropriate and valuable, although it is usually treated too much as a generic type of information-gathering task.

For security, in particular, this practice currently involves requests for information on security policies, security architectural elements, and even specific techniques such as encryption. Such requests are important and should be highlighted for national infrastructure protection projects. The problem is that such inquiries simply do not go far enough. In particular, any organization being considered in a solicitation that involves national infrastructure should provide evidence of at least the following past practices:

- *Past damage*—The organization should be able to provide evidence of past security incidents that it dealt with that produced real malicious damage to some valued asset. Although this might seem paradoxical, the reality is that no organization can claim true skill in securing large infrastructure if it has not dealt with a real incident in the past. Groups who are forthcoming in explaining these past incidents are also generally more mature in their current security processes.

> A mature security organization will admit to successful attacks against them.

- *Past prevention*—Similarly, the organization should be able to provide evidence of incidents prevented. This is tougher than one might think, because in many cases security protections have a preventive effect that is not easily determined or measured. So only the truly skilled security organizations can provide this evidence of deliberate action that prevented an attack from succeeding. A good example might be the establishment of real-time network filtering well in advance of any DDOS attack; if this filtering was actually used to stop an attack attempt, it demonstrates excellent judgment regarding the organizational priorities around security.

> Providing evidence of successful preventive measures is a challenge for most organizations.

- *Past response*—This is the most commonly cited security experience component. Groups can generally point to their response functions as being invoked during worms, viruses, and other attacks.

In any formal project solicitation, these requirements should be highlighted and assigned high priority. Few requirements can properly highlight an organization's ability to handle security situations in the future as their experiences dealing with similar matters in the past.

National Commonality Program

The challenge in creating a new national program of ensuring commonality with state-of-the-art security practices in infrastructure protection involves balancing several different concerns:

- *Plethora of existing standards*—Most organizations are already frustrated with the number of standards and audits that must be covered. The implication is that the creation of a new national security standard commensurate with the six practices described in this chapter would not be well received.
- *Low-water mark versus world class*—As we've discussed, the existing security standards and audits in place today are more focused on creating a common low-water mark, rather than pushing groups to reach for world-class status in security.
- *Existing commissions and boards*—The field is already crowded with national commissions, working groups, and boards comprised of business and government leaders who are working to create sets of recommendations for infrastructure security. They are unlikely to go away and must be factored into any implementation plan.

> Do not try to work around the existing security commissions and boards; instead, factor them into your overall security plans and policies.

While these may not be formal standards with associated audit processes, affected organizations feel the pressure to review these works and to demonstrate some degree of acceptance, if not compliance. The solution to balancing these concerns lies in several implementation approaches and hints that are based on previous experiences with multiple standards and requirements, such as the Orange Book, Red Book, and associated "security rainbow series" in the 1980s. The first is that government really should adopt a single standard for all commercial and government security audits. It really doesn't even matter which audit standard is selected as long as it is *only one*. All subsequent government solicitations and contracts should demand compliance with this standard. Commercial entities might gradually merge toward this standard.

Second, the world-class practices described here should be embedded into all government solicitations and contracts as functional requirements on companies and agencies. This would avoid the problems of audit compliance and would push the security components into the functional category along with performance, processing, storage, and networking. Government agencies could perhaps complement this by rewarding or providing incentives for the inclusion of these requirements in private deals between companies.

DEPTH

Sun myth: If a person is wearing a foundation makeup with SPFs of #4 or #8, then she won't need additional sunscreen or sunblock.
www.ultimate-cosmetics.com

The general security strategy of *defense in depth* is based on the observation that any given layer of protection can fail at any time. As such, defense in depth involves the deliberate introduction of multiple layers of defense in order to increase the likelihood that a given attack will be stopped or at least slowed down. This likelihood is dependent upon the quality and relative attributes of the various defensive layers. Cost and end-user experience issues usually create constraints on just how strong the various layers can actually be in practice. Most security experts understand this strategy of defense in depth, but evidence of its use in national infrastructure settings is often lacking. This is too bad, because the protection of national infrastructure lends itself naturally to multiple layers of defense.

The general schema associated with layered defense is that a series of protective elements is located between an asset and the adversary. Obviously, it would be best if the series is actually that—a serial collection of protective elements that must each be traversed successfully to gain access to a protected resource. Most of the time, however, the layering is not so efficient and may include different combinations of elements between an asset and an adversary. The strategic goals in such cases are to detect and remove any single-layer access paths and, obviously, to avoid situations where the layers might be conflicting. For national infrastructure, the goal is to place multiple security layers in front of all essential services (see Figure 6.1).

The security intent for any series of layers is to enforce policy across all possible access paths to the target asset. Thus, if an asset is accessible through a single entry point, then the layers only need to enforce policy at that point. If an asset is broadly accessible from a collection of different entry points, then the layered defense needs to fan out across these points to enforce policy. Defense in depth methods are said to fail if all of the

Cyber Attacks. DOI: 10.1016/B978-0-12-384917-5.00006-8

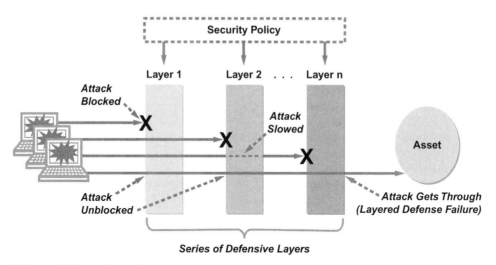

Figure 6.1 General defense in depth schema.

layers do not either block or sufficiently degrade attack attempts at the protected asset, resulting in security policy violations by an adversary. It is relatively easy to determine that a failure has occurred when an attack is detected; however, when an attack goes unnoticed or when the forensic analysis after an attack cannot determine the point of exploitation, then holes in layered defenses might remain indefinitely.

Defense in depth implementations are sometimes inappropriately or even maliciously bypassed by presumably trusted users, generally insiders to a company or agency, including its employees, contractors, and partners. For example, an infrastructure organization might create diverse layers of security functionality to ensure that intruders cannot compromise assets from an external environment such as the Internet. Problems arise, however, if malicious insiders can directly access and compromise assets. This implies that great rigor and discipline are required to ensure that defense in depth truly surrounds an asset, both internally to an organization, as well as externally on the Internet. This generally requires additional functional controls on the local enterprise network to protect assets from insiders.

Depth strategies sometimes involve the familiar military notion of one protection layer slowing down an intruder. It turns out that throttling does not always extrapolate well to cyber security. In practice, cyber security methods tend to be binary in their functionality; that is, a protection will either work or it will not. Debates thus arise around how long an approach will hold off attackers, as in the selection of cryptographic key length.

> If layered defenses are penetrated, it is crucial to identify the entry point used by the attacker.

> Do not overlook the need for protection against both internal and external adversaries.

Similarly, network attacks are often dealt with by throttling or rate-limiting the traffic allowable into a target asset environment. These approaches might work to a degree, but they are the exceptions, and it is recommended that cyber security architectures for national infrastructure not rely on any element having only a partial effect on a given attack.

> Ideal defensive strategies will stop—not slow down—an adversary.

Effectiveness of Depth

Academics formally model the effectiveness of a collection of defensive layers using mathematical probability. Such an approach requires that one quantitatively measure the relative dependencies between the layers, as well as the probability of effectiveness for any given layer. Unfortunately, in any nontrivial environment, both of these estimates are unlikely to be more than just an educated guess. We know, for example, that the success of access controls for enterprise applications is dependent on the success of strong authentication for remote access. Trying to accurately quantify this dependency for probabilistic analysis is a waste of time and will not result in any estimate better than an expert guess.

> How can effectiveness of a security layer be measured or quantified?

Thus, from a practical perspective, and in the context of real national infrastructure protection, determining the effectiveness of a defense in depth scheme must be done via educated guesses. We can make this sound better by referring to it as *informal subjective reasoning based on relevant security factors*, but it is still just a guess. The relevant factors for estimating effectiveness of a layer include the following:

- *Practical experience*—One can certainly analyze practical experience and past results for a given security method. This is dangerous if taken too literally, because many attacks are missed, and seemingly correct, but actually vulnerable, defenses might be dormant for a period of time before an attack.
- *Engineering analysis*—Experienced security engineers will use their knowledge and expertise to provide excellent judgment on whether a given layer will be effective. Vendors and salespeople are to be avoided in this process, because they will invariably distort their product and service capability.
- *Use-case studies*—Providing some rigor to the engineering analysis is a good idea, and the familiar use-case methodology is especially appropriate for security layers. It is really a form of testing.
- *Testing and simulation*—Actual testing of a layer in a controlled setting will provide good information on its effectiveness.

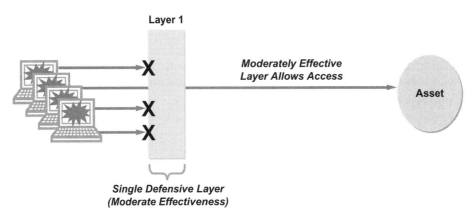

Figure 6.2 Moderately effective single layer of protection.

Simulation is also a good idea in cases where a defensive layer protects against something not easily tested, such as a massive denial of service attack.

To illustrate this approach, let's start with a simple setup, as shown in Figure 6.2. Specifically, a single layer of protection depth is depicted and is estimated to have "moderate" effectiveness. We can assume that some subset of the factors described above was used to make this determination. Maybe some team of experts analyzed the protection, looked at its effectiveness in similar settings, and performed a series of tests and simulations. In any event, let's assume that they decided that a given protection would be moderately effective against the types of attacks to be expected in the local threat environment.

The determination that this single layer is "moderately" effective is nothing more than a subjective guess in most cases. It is, however, an important piece of information for national infrastructure protection because it implies that the protection will not work in all cases; that is, the experts have determined that some types of attacks will bypass or break the protection and will thus expose the asset to malicious intruders. As a result, when a given protection layer does not address all known attacks, then we can conclude the following:

- *Flaws*—The protection might be flawed. This could be some minor issue such as an obscure bug that would allow certain types of attacks or it could be potentially front-page news with major implications. In either case, flaws in protections require either that they be fixed or that they be mitigated by a complementary layer of protection.

- *Suitability*—The protection might be unsuited to the target environment; for example, it might be intended to prevent

> A moderately effective defense strategy will stop most, but not all, attacks.

events A and B in an environment where the real threat is event C. Such scenarios are commonly found during incident response, when some event has occurred and the presumed protections are discovered to have had little effect, simply because of a mismatch. This is fixed by either changing the layer or complementing it with another.

Whether the layer is flawed or mismatched, the situation is made worse if the adversary has knowledge of the situation. Regardless of the common argument by hackers that exposing problems in a protection method should always be reported, the reality is that such information generally does more harm than good. Certainly, if an organization is lax in fixing a problem with broad implications, this is unacceptable, but the technique of extorting that group into taking immediate action is not always in everyone's best interests. The hacker who exposes vulnerabilities in a moderately effective mobile telephony control, for example, without first alerting the service provider, might be guilty of degrading essential communication services that might affect human lives.

> Multiple layers of protection will mitigate the effects of flaws or protections that are unsuited to the target environment.

Assuming an organization is diligent and chooses to improve or fix a moderately effective protection, the result will be that the new estimate or guess might be "highly" effective. For example, suppose that some home-grown intrusion detection system is becoming difficult to maintain. The local team might thus determine that it is only moderately effective and might replace it with a vendor-supported product. In most cases, the new system would now be viewed as highly effective (with the caveat that no intrusion detection systems ever seem to work as well as they should). The end result is that the layer has now been improved from moderately to highly effective. It should be obvious that even in a highly effective protection environment, there will always be exceptional conditions where the protection may fail (see Figure 6.3).

> A protection layer can be improved to become "highly" effective, but no layer is 100% effective all of the time.

Improving one layer is not, however, the only option available. An alternative would be for the moderately effective control to be left in place and complemented with another layer of protection. This has certain advantages, including reducing the cost and risk of forklifting out a security protection layer and replacing it with a new one. The result of complementing one moderately effective protection layer with another is that the end result should mitigate a larger set of attacks. This does introduce an odd sort of calculus to the security manager, where decisions are required around whether some number of moderately effective protections is better or worse than a smaller number of stronger protections (see Figure 6.4).

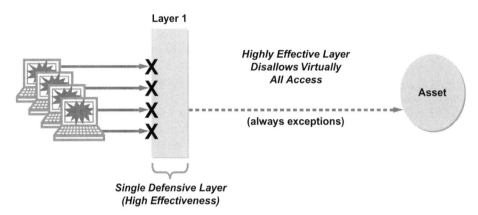

Figure 6.3 Highly effective single layer of protection.

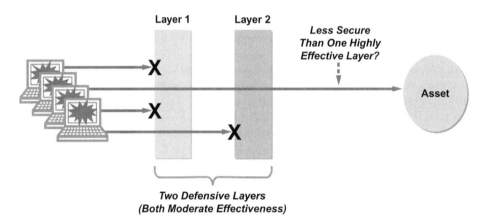

Figure 6.4 Multiple moderately effective layers of protection.

The answer to whether multiple moderately effective layers outperform fewer highly effective ones will depend on aggregation considerations. That is, if two moderate protections complement each other by balancing each respective weakness, then the composite protection will be quite good. If, on the other hand, multiple moderate protections suffer from similar weaknesses, then the weakness will remain in the aggregate protection. In practice, security managers generally should look for a diverse set of protections that are as strong as possible and that balance weaknesses in some demonstrable manner. For national infrastructure protection, this will typically involve layers of protection in authentication, malware protection, access controls, encryption, and intrusion detection.

Diversity of protection layers—including diversity of weaknesses—is critical in maintaining successful protection against attacks.

Layered Authentication

Most information technology (IT) and security teams in government and industry are committed to reducing the number of passwords, passphrases, handheld tokens, certificates, biometrics, and other validation tokens that exist in their environment. These initiatives are generally met with great enthusiasm among end users, because they result in simpler, cleaner infrastructure and much less for end users to have to remember, protect, or write down. One cannot deny that such simplification has a beneficial impact on overall security. For these reasons, various proposals have been made for national authentication systems run by government and that would include every citizen.

Single sign-on (SSO) initiatives are generally used to accomplish this authentication simplification objective. SSO is accomplished by the use of a single, common identification and authentication system for all relevant applications. This common system is then embedded into one identity management process so reported identities can be administered and protected uniformly. The simplification inherent in SSO is desirable from a security perspective, because it reduces the likelihood of errors that result when multiple complex login systems are present. Common identity management is thus generally desirable from a security perspective, especially in enterprise settings.

Problems can arise, however, in national infrastructure protection environments if the process of streamlining authentication goes too far. Even the staunchest advocate of SSO must agree that, for certain applications, a properly managed, properly designed, and diverse series of authentication challenges that are reliant on separate proof factors will be more secure than a comparable SSO system. The diverse series of authentication steps will certainly be less convenient for end users but, if run correctly, will be more secure. This is because such a scheme avoids the nightmarish scenario where a single login provides an adversary with common access across multiple national infrastructure systems. This attack scenario is so unacceptable at the national level that it dictates special consideration.

Specifically, for national infrastructure management, organizations can acceptably maintain the goal of balancing the risks and rewards of SSO for all enterprise-grade applications such as business e-mail, routine applications, and remote access. As long as no national assets can be directly compromised with SSO access, this is fine. Companies and agencies charged with national infrastructure can and should move to an SSO scheme with corresponding identity management. For critical national

> End users will embrace authentication simplification initiatives, and these are certainly easier to monitor from a security management standpoint.

> Single sign-on initiatives may be embraced by end users but may not provide the ideal level of security protection.

services and applications, however, a more complex, defense in depth scheme is highly recommended for end-user authentication (see box).

Factors of a Successful National Infrastructure SSO Access System

Critical national infrastructure services need a defense in depth scheme that is developed with the following considerations:

- *Diversity with single sign-on*—Authentication systems for national asset protection must be different from the SSO scheme used for enterprise access. This implies that a separate technology, vendor, and management process should be considered between enterprise SSO and national infrastructure authentication. The goal is to ensure that flaws in one authentication system are not present in the other.
- *Diversity of proof factors*—Similarly, the familiar proof factors:
  - "Something you know"
  - "Something you have"
  - "Something you embody (biometrics)"
  - "Somewhere you are"

  should be diverse for national assets from any SSO proof factors. This implies that employees should not be handed a single handheld authenticator that can be used to gain access to e-mail and also to some critical infrastructure operational component.
- *Emphasis on security*—While it is acceptable to emphasize usability in enterprise SSO initiatives, the emphasis of national infrastructure protection should shift squarely toward security. The only relevant end-user issues are ones that simplify usage to reduce errors. Convenience should not necessarily be a major goal, as long as the authentication scheme does not drive bad behavior such as sharing tokens or writing down passwords.

> Single sign-in access can be part of a multilayered defense in depth strategy.

A resultant typical defense in depth scheme for national infrastructure organizations would include SSO for enterprise-grade applications and access and a subsequent, diverse authentication process for all national assets. The result is that end users would need to be authenticated twice before gaining access to a critical asset. Correspondingly, intruders would have to break through two authentication systems to gain malicious access to the target asset. End users probably would not like this and the costs are higher, but the increased security is worth the trouble (see Figure 6.5).

For multiple critical national assets in an infrastructure environment, the depth strategy should include maximal diversity for each asset. That is, the general computing characteristics

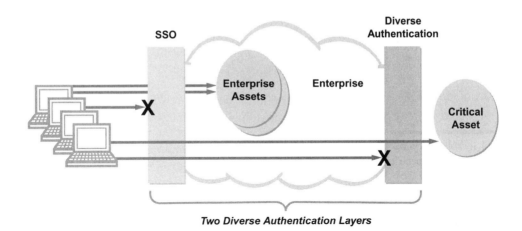

Figure 6.5 Schema showing two layers of end-user authentication.

and source of the authentication functionality should be diverse. Furthermore, the factors used in establishing proof of identity for critical assets should be stronger than simple passwords; handheld authentication or biometrics would be recommended. An implication here is that the underlying infrastructure be operated with the greatest precision and correctness. Administrative procedures for obtaining an authentication token, restoring access when a token or password is lost, and providing assistance to confused end users must be carefully designed to avoid social engineering attacks. At the national level, this would require frequent testing.

A key modern consideration for enterprise authentication is the degree to which mobile access to infrastructure potentially changes security posture. As an example, consider that most organizations go to great lengths to ensure that several layers of authentication reside between remote workers and sensitive applications such as enterprise e-mail. In fact, see the box to follow the experience most people have when trying to get their enterprise e-mail from a remote location using a laptop.

The example in the box also highlights the importance of recognizing trends in technology as national infrastructure protection initiatives are considered. For the enterprise, the old notion of protected perimeter thus disappears with the advent of mobile access across wireless carrier infrastructure. One still finds architectures where users must "hairpin" their mobile access to the enterprise and then through a firewall to the target application, but this practice is likely to wane (see Figure 6.6).

> Unfortunately, mobile devices eliminate the multi-layered protection most companies build into their remote network access.

Multi-Layered Protection: Five Steps to Remote E-Mail Access

A typical remote worker will need to follow these steps to access their enterprise e-mail account:

- *Authentication layer 1.* The user must first login to the computer. Presumably, this is done using a password that is set by the enterprise information technology or security group.
- *Authentication layer 2.* The user must then login to the local WiFi or broadband access network. Sometimes this is free; other times it requires a credit card, which can be viewed as an added identification step.
- *Authentication layer 3.* The user must then login to the remote access server, probably over a virtual private network (VPN). Most of the time, companies and agencies require a personal identification number (PIN), password, or handheld token to authenticate VPN access.
- *Authentication layer 4.* The user must then login to the enterprise network, probably with some sort of domain password. This is also controlled by the local information technology or security group.
- *Authentication layer 5.* The user must finally login to the specific e-mail application being used by the enterprise. Sometimes this requires another password, but often it just requires access.

On the surface, this would seem like the ultimate in layered authentication with no less than five layers! The problem is that many organizations provide their employees with means to remotely access applications such as e-mail with a handheld device. Consider, in this case, the experience most people have when trying to retrieve their enterprise e-mail using a mobile device:

- *Authentication layer 1.* The user must simply login to the mobile device, click on the e-mail icon, and then read or create mail.

This is obviously only one layer of authentication for mobile devices, and it demonstrates the importance of recognizing that users might find more convenient paths around presumed layers of authentication.

For applications such as enterprise e-mail, this type of convenient bypass might be perfectly fine. In fact, for enterprise e-mail specifically, it would be unreasonable to expect that workers in national infrastructure settings should not be allowed mobile access. For more sensitive national infrastructure applications, however, such as those that provision or control critical systems, a threat analysis would be required before any alternative paths with mobile devices are allowed. Classified information would be another example asset that requires multiple layers without mobile access bypass. These types of requirements should find their way into any type of national infrastructure support contracts.

> Exposing critical national assets to mobile access (even by trusted personnel) opens a gateway for an adversarial attack.

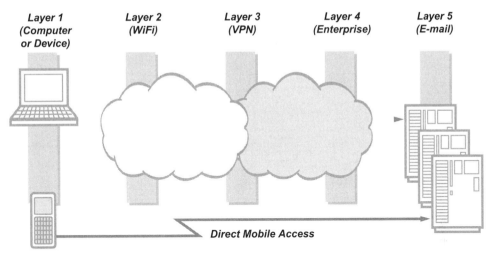

Figure 6.6 Authentication options including direct mobile access.

Layered E-Mail Virus and Spam Protection

Commercial environments are increasingly turning to virtualized, in-the-cloud solutions for their gateway filtering of e-mail viruses and spam. This decision allows the organization to remove the gateway filters or to simply offload the work those filters must perform. This is a healthy decision, because a general security principle is that attacks should be stopped as close as possible to their source. The network is certainly closer than the attack target's ingress point, so virtual filtering is desirable. It is also helpful to the carrier, because it reduces the junk floating around network infrastructure, which helps carriers perform their tasks more efficiently in support of national services.

Managers of commercial environments have also come to recognize that their computing end points cannot rely solely on gateway or in-the-cloud processing. As such, the state of the practice in e-mail virus and spam protection involves a defense in depth deployment of filters to each laptop, netbook, personal computer, and server in the enterprise. The approach is even beginning to find its way to the mobile handheld device, where the threat of viruses and spam is increasing. As such, a given virus or spam e-mail sent from a malicious source will have to find its way through at least two layers of filtering in order to reach its intended source (see Figure 6.7).

This cloud filtering arrangement found in most companies is acceptable for organizations charged with national

Mobile devices are susceptible to viruses and spam, yet spam is more of a nuisance than an actual threat to national infrastructure.

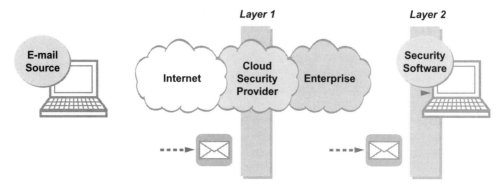

Figure 6.7 Typical architecture with layered e-mail filtering.

infrastructure. For the most critical applications, it is recommended that a depth approach involving both in-the-cloud and perimeter processing be employed. In addition, for key executives in these companies and agencies who might be directly targeted by adversaries, additional desktop and application filtering might be prudent. Practical experience suggests that spam is more a nuisance than significant threat to national asset management, so the likelihood of attackers using spam to interrupt national services is only moderate. In addition, antivirus software has become less relevant in recent years, simply because so many software threats such as well-coded bots are not easily detected by antivirus software. Research into better techniques for detecting the presence of malware should become an immediate national priority.

> Antivirus software, while still necessary, is not likely to detect such threats as a botnet attack.

Layered Access Controls

Access controls determine who can access what resources under which conditions. They are one of the most common and most mature security protection methods, dating back to the earliest electronic computers. If some asset is protected by a single set of access controls, then this is similar to using a single combination lock to protect a physical asset. That is, if an individual has the correct combination, then access is allowed. Common access controls include access control lists (ACLs) on Windows®-based operating systems and permissions vectors in UNIX®-based operating systems. These are implemented as software data structures that determine access based on some defined policy.

One approach to using defense in depth to protect a software application involves embedding one type of access control into the application environment and then hosting the application on an operating system that utilizes a different type of access control. In such a setup, access to the application can only be obtained by successfully negotiating the following layers:

- *Access control layer 1.* The user must be permitted entry to the operating system via the operating system access controls. This might be UNIX® permissions, Windows® ACLs, or something similar.
- *Access control layer 2.* The user must be permitted entry to the application via the application access controls. This is likely to be a password embedded in the application environment and controlled by the application owner.

In cases where an operating system and application cannot be remotely reached, these two layers can be augmented with additional diverse controls such as guarded access to the physical premise or to a locked data center. This implies that access to an application would require first obtaining physical access to a console before access to the operating system and application can even be attempted. These two layers of authentication are important and should be tested in every national infrastructure environment, especially ones employing supervisory control and data acquisition (SCADA), where computer security techniques have a more short-lived legacy. A caution, however, is that insiders are likely to possess both types of access, so the layers will not be helpful in stopping most forms of sabotage.

In cases where remote access is allowed, then the use of a firewall is the most common method to ensure policy compliance for those permitted access. Such policy is almost always based on the source Internet protocol (IP) address of the requesting party. This is not the strongest of access control methods, simply because IP addresses are so easily spoofed. Also, to maintain such a scheme, a complex and potentially error-prone or socially engineered bureaucracy must be put in place that accepts and maintains access requests. When used in conjunction with additional access control layers such as operating system and application controls, the result might be acceptable in some environments (see Figure 6.8).

For national infrastructure protection, critical assets should be covered by as many layers of access control as deemed feasible. As with authentication, the issue of end-user convenience must be viewed as lower priority if critical national services are at stake. Some general heuristics for protecting national infrastructure with layered access controls include the following:

- *Network-based firewalls*—Using cloud firewalls offers an additional blanket layer of control. This technique is useful as a complement to existing enterprise controls, especially because

> Some form of access control is present in any network connection (e.g., your personal password to access your e-mail account).

> Restricting physical access to assets always adds another layer of protection from outsiders, but not from internal saboteurs.

> The implementation of layered access controls places greater emphasis on protection than on end-user convenience.

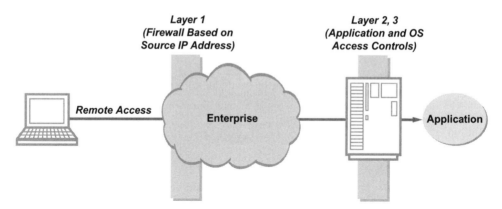

Figure 6.8 Three layers of protection using firewall and access controls.

carrier-based systems will generally differ from whatever firewalls and related systems might be deployed in the enterprise.

- *Internal firewalls*—This provides yet another layer of protection within the enterprise to ensure that individuals with access to resource *X* only gain access to that resource and no other. Routers can often provide a simple packet-filtering capability as part of their native processing suite, which simplifies architecture and minimizes cost.
- *Physical security*—Excellent facility and premise-access security provides an additional tangible layer of protection and is essential for any national infrastructure protection initiatives. This must be complemented by selecting suitable applications and systems that can never be accessed remotely or even across a local area network.

Multiple access control systems must be well managed so as not to allow an internal attacker successful infiltration to the systems.

When multiple access control systems are in place, the benefit of layering is reduced when the underlying administration function is performed by one team using a common set of tools. When this involves a protected and carefully managed security operations center the situation is acceptable, but when the management is *ad hoc* and poorly controlled the layering might be undermined by an attacker who successfully infiltrates the administration systems.

Layered Encryption

Encryption is an effective and well-known security control for protecting information. While mathematicians and computer scientists have created hundreds of different taxonomies for categorizing symmetric and public key systems, the box shows specific methods that are useful for the protection of national infrastructure.

Five Encryption Methods for National Infrastructure Protection

1. *Mobile device storage*—Mobile smart phones and laptops should have native encryption to protect against loss or theft and the resulting information compromise. The encryption will never be perfect but should provide useful protection in the field. Several vendors offer this type of encryption as an add-on service, but this should eventually become a native function in all mobile devices and laptops.

2. *Network transmission*—Any sensitive data being transmitted within an enterprise or between knowing partners should be encrypted. The traditional means for such encryption has been symmetric and embedded in hardware devices. More recently, the associated cryptography is often software based and involves public keys supported by public key infrastructure (PKI) tools. When network transmission occurs in an *ad hoc* manner, the practical consideration is that shared cryptography simply does not exist between organizations due to complexity. This makes it difficult to encrypt network traffic without coordinating things in advance.

3. *Secure commerce*—If an organization offers electronic commerce services over the Internet, the use of common encryption techniques such as Secure Sockets Layer (SSL) is presumed. The associated cryptography here will be public key based.

4. *Application strengthening*—E-mail is the most obvious application that can introduce secrecy and authentication properties via the use of encryption. As noted above, federating this cryptography, almost always public key based, between organizations has not been done on a wide scale to date.

5. *Server and mainframe data storage*—Encryption on servers and mainframes has received considerable attention in recent years but should be viewed with suspicion. Data at rest is poorly protected by cryptography because the associated key management systems, which require a long life, can have obvious holes. In the worst case, sloppy key management can make data less secure. Note that smart phones and laptops are different from servers because they are *moving*.

The good news is that, for the most part, these five encryption methods will not collide in practice. They can be used in combination and in cooperation, with no great functional or administrative problems expected. It is also perfectly fine to encrypt information multiple times, as long as the supporting administrative tools are working properly. As such, one can easily imagine scenarios where all five systems are in place and provide five different layers of information protection. Not all will typically reside in a perfect series, but all can be in place in one infrastructure setting providing layered security (see Figure 6.9).

> Information can be encrypted multiple times to achieve layered protection.

The bad news, however, is that each will typically require its own user administration and key management systems. The result is a disparate view of cryptography across the enterprise that can be seen in the somewhat scattered arrangement in

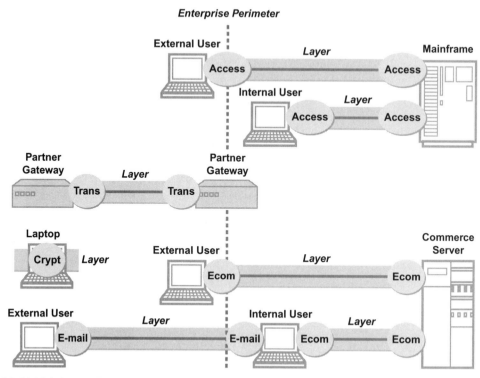

Figure 6.9 Multiple layers of encryption.

Figure 6.9. This is unfortunate, because it increases complexity, which increases the chances of error or compromise, especially to underlying infrastructure. Regardless, the use of cryptography in national infrastructure protection should be encouraged, even if the layers are not optimally coordinated.

Layered Intrusion Detection

Intrusion detection was once viewed as the most promising of large-scale security techniques. Even the provocative and hopeful name "intrusion detection" suggests a powerful technology that can be inserted into an environment to alert security teams when an intrusion is imminent. While this goal has not been fully met in practice, intrusion detection does provide a useful means for detecting indicators of potentially harmful behavior. These indicators are sometimes used for early warning, but more often are used to correlate with other types of available information during an incident.

Because intrusion detection is typically performed offline, it lends itself to multiple layers of monitoring. Obviously, if the intrusion detection includes an active response—which is referred to collectively as *intrusion prevention*—the layered arrangement could be more complex, but for now let's analyze strategies for passive, offline monitoring of attack. Most organizations accomplish this task using commercial systems that include three components: monitors that are placed in strategic locations to collect data, transmission systems that move alarm information to a central location, and a master monitoring function that processes incoming data and provides some sort of correlated summary, usually in the form of an alarm to a console. When this type of intrusion detection system is in place in an enterprise, it can be viewed as an explicit layer of protection. In fact, many auditors will accept intrusion detection as a complementary control when some other protection displays weaknesses.

> Intrusion detection with data security is similar to physical security intrusion detection: monitoring, an alarm system, and a central console.

One can conceptualize an alternate layer of intrusion detection being put in place at a broader level, perhaps coordinated by some government or industry group. The components of the system would be the same, but differences from the enterprise would include diverse monitor placement, different signatures of attack, and a broader base on which to perform correlation of data. An issue with this alternative layer is that the protection would likely involve network paths that are largely separate from those in specific enterprise settings. For example, an intrusion aimed at some government agency would not be detected by the intrusion detection system located within a separate enterprise. There are, however, three specific opportunities for different intrusion detection systems to provide layered protection:

- *In-band detection*—If two intrusion detection systems both have monitoring access to the same attack stream, or a related one, then they might both have the opportunity to detect the condition. Thus, if one system fails, it is possible that another might not. This is the essence of defense in depth, but it only works if the response processes for each detection system are coordinated.
- *Out-of-band correlation*—During an incident, the operators of an intrusion detection system might benefit from information that might become available from other operators. This can be intelligence about sources, methods, or techniques being used by attackers. It is usually best used if made available in real time.
- *Signature sharing*—A special case of the above correlation involves sharing of specific attack signatures by one operator that can be keyed into the systems being run by other

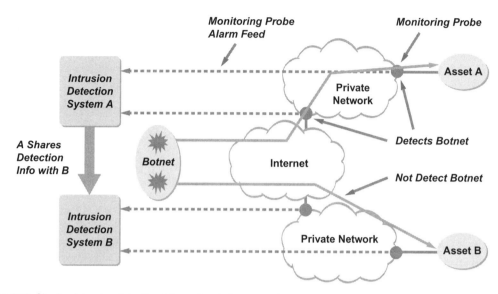

Figure 6.10 Sharing intrusion detection information between systems.

operators. Military organizations, for example, sometimes develop signatures that could be shared with industrial groups to improve their security.

In each of these cases, diverse intrusion detection systems can be viewed as providing a defense in depth for target assets. The result is a potentially coordinated series of intrusion detection layers that will help protect national infrastructure. This coordination usually requires sharing between different monitoring and analysis centers; that is, if one intrusion detection system notices an attack such as a botnet, then it might share this information with another system that might not have detected the condition (see Figure 6.10).

This idea of coordinated intrusion detection systems is certainly not new; for example, government cyber security commissions and groups have advocated the notion of signature sharing between government and industry for years. For whatever reason, however, such coordination has rarely occurred, but for national infrastructure protection to reach its full potential such cooperation must be encouraged and rewarded.

> A certain amount of information sharing between government agencies may serve to increase intrusion detection effectiveness.

National Program of Depth

Creating a coordinated program of defense in depth using multiple layers of security for national infrastructure can only be ensured via careful architectural analysis of all assets and protection systems. The architectural analysis should result in a mapping, perhaps represented as a matrix, where each critical national asset is shown to be protected by certain multiple layers of security. For each layer, subjective determination of its effectiveness is also required. Once this is done, simple calculations can be performed to determine the difficulty of penetration through the various layers. This task is easier than it sounds; some of the more practical considerations that arise in such an exercise include the following:

- *Identifying assets*—This is a required step for several of our recommended national infrastructure protection principles, including, for example, deception. It is particularly important for defense in depth, because the analysis of depth effectiveness can only be measured from the specifically identified assets.

- *Subjective estimations*—The challenges inherent in this step were explained in detail above; certainly, in practice, certain conventions could arise that would help security experts arrive at common estimations of effectiveness. In the 1980s, the U.S. Department of Defense created a set of criteria (informally called the Orange Book) for measuring the effectiveness of security in systems. Perhaps some elements of this criteria approach could be introduced to provide assistance in subjective estimations of the effectiveness of a layer.

- *Obtaining proprietary information*—If a company or agency has some defense in place (or, more importantly, perhaps some defense that may be missing) for some essential national service, then obtaining this information for broad analysis may be difficult. The goal would be to demonstrate value for organizations sharing detailed information, even if it is bad news.

- *Identifying all possible access paths*—Perhaps the toughest part of any cyber security exercise involves trying to determine means for accessing some target. If this is not done properly, then the defense in depth strategy will fall apart, so this important step requires special consideration.

These considerations can introduce significant challenges in practice. It does not help that most existing security teams, even in large-scale settings, rarely go through a local exercise of identifying defense in depth conditions. As a result, most national infrastructure protection teams would be working this exercise for the first time in the context of a national program.

> Reviewing systems and strategies to identify existing layers of protection will create a "map" of the current depth of defensive protection.

DISCRETION

The British spook said it on the way to the pub—a seemingly random confession that stood out in contrast to the polite evasions that were Ellis's standard form of reply. Public key cryptography? "You did a lot more with it than we did," he said.

Steven Levy[1]

A belief found occasionally in the hacking community is that all information should be free and that anyone trying to suppress information flow is evil. The problem with this view is that it suggests that sensitive personal data should be exposed to the world. As such, this extreme view is commonly modified by hackers as follows: All information associated with *organizations*, especially government, should be free, but private data about individuals should never be disclosed. From a logical perspective, this is a curious distinction, because large organizations are comprised of individuals, but in practice the view makes perfect sense. Hackers are almost universally concerned with protecting the rights of the individual; this view of information establishes a charter for the hacking community to make public anything that might degrade individual rights.

The result is a hacking culture where it is considered acceptable to expose proprietary information from government and industry in hacking magazines, on websites, at conferences, and across the Internet. Hackers often claim that reporting commercial and national vulnerabilities is a useful public service that prompts a more rapid security fix. This certainly does not justify leaking proprietary information that has nothing to do with vulnerabilities, but it does offer some value—albeit in an overly forceful manner. Regardless of the motivation, the fact is that proprietary information in companies and agencies will most definitely be widely exposed if discovered by hackers. Perhaps worse, terrorists and information warriors are also interested in

[1] S. Levy, The open secret: public key cryptography—the breakthrough that revolutionized email and ecommerce—was first discovered by American geeks. Right? Wrong, *Wired*, 7(4), 1999.

Cyber Attacks. DOI: 10.1016/B978-0-12-384917-5.00007-X

this information, but for more malicious purposes—and they will rarely make their intentions public in advance.

The result is that national infrastructure protection initiatives must include means for protecting sensitive information from being leaked. The best approach is to avoid vulnerabilities in the first place, as this information is the most urgently sought and valuable for public disclosure. More practically, however, national infrastructure includes a wide spectrum of information ranging from innocuous tidbits and gossip to critically sensitive data about infrastructure. This spectrum requires a customized protection program focused primarily on the most critical information. Any practical implementation should therefore combine mandatory, functional security controls with programs that dictate the use of *discretion* by individuals possessing important information. Mandatory controls can be implemented centrally, but discretion must be embedded in the local culture and followed in a distributed and individualized manner.

> Exposure of vulnerabilities can force a quick response, but that same exposure might lead adversaries directly to private data.

Trusted Computing Base

The nearest the computer security community has come to recognizing the importance of human discretion lies in an architectural construct introduced in the 1980s called a *trusted computing base* (TCB). The definition of TCB is the totality of hardware, software, processes, and individuals whose correct operation and decision-making are considered essential to the overall security of the system. In an operating system, this would include the system files and processes in the underlying kernel. In an organization, this would include the system and security administrators who operate the critical protection systems. For an organization, it would also include all constructs for managing and storing personally identifiable information (PII) about employees and customers. Candidates for exclusion from a TCB include anything whose malfunction or public disclosure would not create a significant or cascading problem. In modern infrastructure, the TCB generally extends to the systems and networks of partner and supplier groups. This greatly complicates the protection of TCB assets because it extends the TCB perimeter to an environment that is more difficult to control.

> A modern TCB extends beyond a single organization, making protection all the more difficult.

The primary goal of any program of discretion in national infrastructure protection should be to ensure that information about TCB functionality, operations, and processes is not exposed inappropriately to anyone not properly authorized and to avoid disclosure to anyone who does not possess a clear business need for that information. Such a program will combine two distinct components:

- *Mandatory controls*—These are the functional and procedural mechanisms that are put in place to ensure that information is protected from unauthorized access. Other than key administrators within the TCB, no individual in any organization should be able to bypass mandatory controls, which will typically include firewalls, intrusion detection systems, and honey pots.
- *Discretionary policy*—These are the rules, recommendations, and guidelines that are put in place by an organization to protect its information, especially with respect to the TCB. The discretion here is generally driven by practical concerns; for example, no functional mechanism can control what people mention informally to colleagues or customers. The only way to ensure protection here is the discretionary guidance afforded by the local culture. This can certainly be complemented with severe punishments if someone clearly violates the spirit of protection for TCB-related information.

As one might expect, the TCB is easiest to protect if its size and complexity are minimized. Having fewer people that must be trusted to support security, for example, is better than having to trust many different people and groups. Similarly, the fewer the systems one must trust in some base, and the less complex these systems are, the better off an organization will be from a security perspective. So, the minimization of a TCB is an excellent goal, albeit one that is often ignored in practice. Security practice has all too often involved the introduction of some new security system that is large and complex and requires full trust (see Figure 7.1).

> A smaller, less complex TCB is much easier to protect.

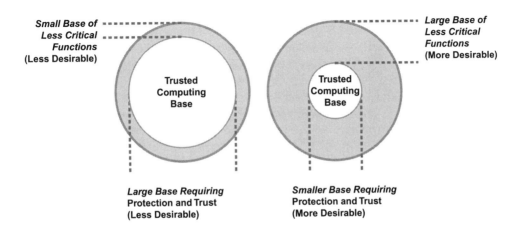

Figure 7.1 Size comparison issues in a trusted computing base.

A major consideration in the protection of national infrastructure thus becomes how to manage, promote, and ensure proper human discretion around critical information related to TCB assets. This requires that policies, procedures, and even functional controls be put in place to assist in exercising such discretion. The idea is that, before any TCB-related information is disclosed that could have an impact on the security of some national asset, the following types of questions must be considered:

> Asking the right questions can help determine the impact of TCB security-related disclosures.

- *Assistance*—Could this information assist an adversary in attacking some aspect of national infrastructure? For example, if terrorists or country-sponsored information warriors had this information, could they mount a malicious campaign against services such as emergency 911?
- *Fixes*—Does disclosure of this information assist in identifying a timelier or more effective security fix? For example, will this disclosure provide someone with information that can reduce the time required to fix the problem?
- *Limits*—Can the information disclosure be limited to those in a position to design a security fix? More specifically, can the disclosure be done quietly and in private to a targeted group such as the vendor or service provider that can directly solve the problem?
- *Legality*—Is disclosure of this information a legal or contractual requirement in the local environment? Or, is this disclosure being done for some other reason—perhaps personal gain or pent-up anger with some organization for moving too slowly?
- *Damage*—Is any individual or group harmed or damaged by protection and nondisclosure of this information?
- *Need*—Do others need this information to protect their own systems or infrastructure?

As suggested, proper human discretion in the interpretation of these questions, along with subsequent decision-making, is critical to protecting national assets. In many cases, government organizations will demand information related to some national infrastructure component or service, especially if the information relates to some trusted computing base. This is fine, as long as the purpose of sharing is reasonable and focused on improving the situation. When such information is demanded by a government group for unspecified purposes (or, at worst, for the purpose of power or gossip), then such sharing is not recommended.

> Before sharing critical information, consider who is requesting it and what the purpose is behind their request.

In any event, regardless of the security process, architectures, and systems put in place to protect assets, humans will remain a critical link in the chain. In fact, in many environments, they may be the weakest link. This is why the exercising of discretion in sharing information is such an important principle.

Security Through Obscurity

A barrier to proper discretion is the much maligned and poorly understood notion of *security through obscurity*. Ask any security expert what they think of this concept, and you will receive a religious argument, especially from cryptographers, that deliberately hiding information to ensure security will not work. Their claim is that anyone trying to hide design, implementation, or operational detail is probably just trying to conceal flaws. Furthermore, all information presumably finds its way public, they will argue, and any dependencies on suppression will eventually topple. The most objectionable applications of security through obscurity can be described in the following two scenarios:

> There are many opponents of security through obscurity as a meaningful protection strategy.

- *Long-term hiding of vulnerabilities*—This involves the operators of a system concealing the existence of some exploitable flaw as their primary, long-term means for securing the system, as opposed to the more desirable approach in which the vulnerability would be removed.
- *Long-term suppression of information*—This involves the operators of a target system deliberately suppressing general information about a system to make things more difficult for adversaries, hackers, and third parties to discover potential flaws in a system.

In each of these scenarios, the primary control involves hiding information. Most would agree that this is not a reliable long-term method, because suppressed information has a tendency to eventually become public. The situation can be depicted as a knowledge time line, where zero information is initially made public about some system. With time, a gradual increase will occur in available public knowledge. If this increase reaches the point where sufficient information is available to mount an exploit, then the security through obscurity scheme has failed. Obviously, disruptive events such as hacker announcements can create abrupt increases in knowledge (see Figure 7.2).

Although security through obscurity is not recommended for long-term protection as a primary control, it remains an excellent complementary control in many cases, as well as being an essential requirement in the short term for many types of security problems in infrastructure. For example, there are no compelling reasons for information about some organization's security architecture to be made public. As long as the security

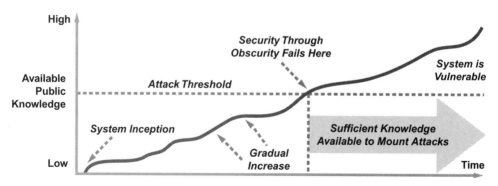

Figure 7.2 Knowledge lifecycle for security through obscurity.

> Security through obscurity should not be a primary protective strategy but can certainly be part of a defense package.

design receives expert local treatment, it is best left not publicized. Certainly, no one should recommend this as a primary control, and it should not be used to hide flaws, but such discretion raises the bar against adversaries and might be the difference between an attack that succeeds and one that fails.

Correspondingly, when some exploitable flaw is discovered locally that requires immediate attention, the worst thing that can happen is for that information to be shared broadly. When this occurs, perhaps as a result of a posting to the Internet, the local response becomes distorted by concerns related to public relations, imminent threat, and legal concerns. Engineering solutions would be much improved if the flaw can be analyzed carefully and embedded into proper development and operations lifecycles. In addition, suppose that the steady state for some system is that sufficient security exists to ensure proper operation, and any vulnerability that might exist is sufficiently obscure as to make the technology reasonably dependable. If a severe vulnerability is then found, the result is that the new steady state could jump to an unacceptably high risk state, and the integrity and dependability of the operation could be in jeopardy. This is simply not acceptable, even for short periods of time, for essential national services.

> Essential national services cannot afford to be in a high risk state, even for a short period of time.

The familiar argument that hackers often make here is that by exposing the vulnerability, a fix is rushed into place. In addition, when the fix is embedded into the original system, the integrity of that system has, by definition, been increased, simply because an existing flaw has been removed. This is a powerful argument and is in fact a correct one. The problem is that for essential services, the vulnerability period—during which risk grows higher than some tolerable threshold—must be avoided. Cold logic generally goes out the window when a service must be in place

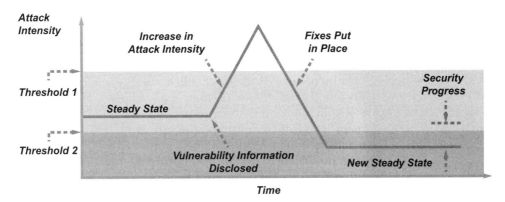

Figure 7.3 Vulnerability disclosure lifecycle.

to ensure that a heart attack victim receives aid, or that tenants in an inner city receive electricity and heat, or that operators of a nuclear power plant can avoid dangerous emergency situations that could create serious health disasters (see Figure 7.3).

Regardless of the specific steady-state attack intensities and acceptable thresholds, the requirement is that the individuals charged with protecting vulnerability information must exercise proper discretion to ensure a level of obscurity for their systems. Without such discretion and obscurity, the chances are great that attack intensities can exceed desired levels, thus leading to serious problems. In general, the practice should be to avoid public disclosure of vulnerabilities until a responsible fix has been put in place. This suggests that disclosure of vulnerability information must be minimized and confined to those in a position to design and embed a proper solution.

Information Sharing

Sensitive information can be exposed in different ways, including deliberate leaks, stray comments, document theft, and hacker disclosure. Each of these occurrences can be jolting for a security team, and their potential creates a general feeling of unease, especially in national infrastructure settings. An additional path for the exposure of sensitive information involves willful information sharing with some controlled, authoritative group. While this is a predictable event, and the recipients are usually delighted with the information, the group doing the sharing is rarely pleased with the overall process.

Information sharing may be inadvertent (stray comments), secretive (document theft), or willful (federal regulations or audits).

Government agencies are the most aggressive in promoting information sharing. Obviously, where legal requirements dictate reporting of data, there is no reason for debate. Law enforcement groups and federal regulators, for example, regularly demand information, but this is done under extremely controlled conditions and rarely, if ever, results in vulnerability-related data being disclosed to an adversary. For cyber security, however, government agencies request that industry share sensitive information for the following reasons:

- *Government assistance to industry*—In theory, attack signatures and related security data could be provided by government to industry, as long as government is fully aware of the vulnerabilities that might reside in commercial infrastructure. This requires information sharing from companies to government.
- *Government situational awareness*—For government to properly assess cyber security risk at the national level, information sharing from industry is required, as such a large portion of national infrastructure resides in industry.
- *Politics*—Government groups are political by nature, and sensitive information provided by industry serves as a type of "power currency" that is used to push political objectives within government. This is rarely stated, but no government official would deny its validity.

In practice, information sharing between industry and government tends to provide spotty results for both parties. The idea of government providing direct cyber security assistance to industry, for example, is mostly theoretical. Valid scenarios can easily be imagined, especially for attack signatures that might be known by a military or intelligence group, but the practical realization of this is rarely seen. Similarly, the idea of government using shared information to form an aggregate view of national cyber security risk sounds great, but has never been done—at least in any public way. In contrast, the political objective has been the primary driver for most information sharing initiatives, which helps explain the enthusiasm that remains in government for this activity. This is a shame, because of all the motivations this one is the least important to the operator sharing data. In fact, an inverse relationship seems to exist between the respective measures of value to the sharing and receiving parties (see Figure 7.4).

> Government and industry are not mutually invested in information sharing for the same reason.

The relationship illustrated in Figure 7.4 shows that whereas government primarily seeks political power with information, industry cares the least about this; correspondingly, where industry would benefit most from government assistance, this

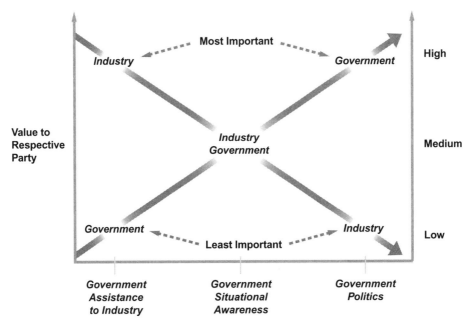

Figure 7.4 Inverse value of information sharing for government and industry.

is an area where government is in the weakest position to help. Both government and industry would agree that it is moderately important that government maintain situation awareness of vulnerabilities, but neither would list this as their primary objective. It is this inverse relationship that helps one understand why information sharing initiatives have rarely worked. It also goes without saying that any cases where information has been shared with government and is then sloppily handled, perhaps even leaked to the press, just makes matters worse.

Certainly, poor handling of sensitive or private information lessens industry's trust in government when sharing information on vulnerabilities.

The recommendation here is that any energy available for expenditure in this area should focus on flattening the two curves somewhat. Government should be less focused on politics, and industry should be less concerned with getting something in return for sharing. The end result is that sharing objectives will naturally converge to an agreed-upon situational awareness objective, which is important but certainly not so important as to warrant all the attention this issue brings to the cyber security discussion.

Information Reconnaissance

Reconnaissance activity performed by an adversary is another means by which sensitive information can be exposed. This is important to recognize because attacks on national infrastructure will always include some form of reconnaissance. It can be done at arm's length using remote access over the Internet; it can be done using compromised or planted insiders with access to critical local data; it can be done using social engineering techniques; it can be done via deliberate theft, remote hacking, or quiet sabotage, and so on. Regardless of the technique or vantage point, reconnaissance is used to plan and prepare for attacks on infrastructure.

> Adversarial attacks are rarely spontaneous; some amount of planning goes into each attack.

Reconnaissance Planning Levels

Three levels of reconnaissance are followed in most instances of cyber attack planning:

1. The first level involves broad, wide-reaching collection from a variety of possible sources. This can include web searches, personal contact, and business interaction.
2. The second level of reconnaissance involves targeted collection, often involving automation to provide assistance. Network scanning is the most common functional support for this second level of reconnaissance.
3. The third level involves direct access to the target. A successful hacking break-in to some system, followed by the collection of targeted data, is an example.

One possible scenario that strings the three phases together might involve broad reconnaissance, where something found on the Internet would prompt more targeted reconnaissance, which would involve the scanning activity to find something that could then be used in the third phase for direct access to a target (see Figure 7.5).

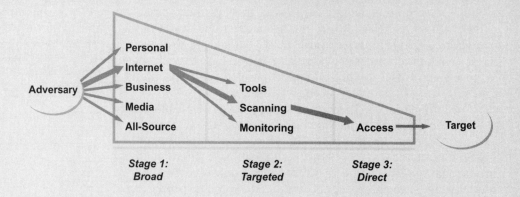

Figure 7.5 Three stages of reconnaissance for cyber security.

This three-stage model suggests that at each layer of information collection by an adversary the opportunity exists for security engineers to introduce information obscurity. The purpose of the obscurity would be to try to prevent a given type of information from being disclosed through the reconnaissance activity. The specific types of security-related national infrastructure information that should be obscured are as follows:

- *Attributes*—This is information about seemingly nonsecurity-related features, functions, and characteristics of the computing, networking, applications, and software associated with national infrastructure. It could include equipment type, vendor name, size and capacity, and supported functionality. Adversaries often covet this type of information because it helps provide context for a given attack.
- *Protections*—This is information related to the security protection of a national asset. It can range from technical configuration or setup data about systems to nontechnical contact information for key security administrative staff. The value of this information should be obvious; when obtained, it provides a roadmap for the type of countermeasures an adversary must consider in planning a successful attack.
- *Vulnerabilities*—This is information related to exploitable holes in national infrastructure. It can range from well-known bugs in commercial operating systems to severe vulnerabilities in some national asset. Adversaries will seek this type of information from any possible source. This can include the national infrastructure management team, relevant technology or service vendors, or even the general public. The hacking community is also a rich source of vulnerability information, especially as it relates to national assets.

Of these three attributes, vulnerability information tends to dominate most discussions about the types of information an adversary might desire. Go to the technical section of any bookstore, for example, and you can find thick tomes chronicling the exploitable holes in virtually any technology you can imagine. This gives you some idea of how difficult it really is to obscure vulnerability information. This should not discourage the operators of national infrastructure; when serious problems are discovered that can degrade essential services, the only responsible action is to work toward some sort of fix with the responsible parties before the information is shared to the rest of the world, which obviously includes the adversary.

> Although truly obscuring vulnerability information is likely an impossibility, security managers should strive for discretion and privacy on this point whenever possible.

Obscurity Layers

One conceptual approach to managing discretion in protecting national infrastructure information involves *obscurity layers*.

Layering the methods of obscurity and discretion adds depth to a defensive security program.

These layers are intended to reduce the likelihood that critical information is disclosed to unauthorized individuals. Techniques for introducing layers of obscurity range from common-sense human discretion to more structured processes for controlling information flow. If designed properly, obscurity layers should make unauthorized disclosure possible only if multiple, diverse obscurity techniques are somehow bypassed. In this sense, obscurity layers can be viewed as an instance of defense in depth.

In the best case, obscurity layers provide diverse, complementary, and efficient coverage around national asset information. That is, an asset might first be protected by an obscurity layer that includes data markings to remind individuals of their obligation to use discretion. A second obscurity layer might involve some mandate that no technical information about local networks, software, or computing platforms be shared beyond the team of trusted administrators. A third layer of obscurity might then involve the mandate that, if information does somehow leak out about critical infrastructure, the organization will never comment publicly on any aspect of the leak.

These three example layers are complementary and provide guidance to individuals on how to exercise discretion in what information to share and what information to suppress. As such, they can be viewed as an effective discretionary tool for protecting assets (see Figure 7.6).

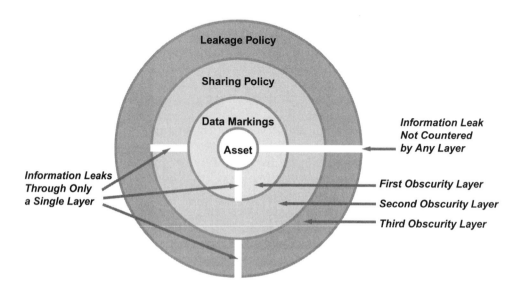

Figure 7.6 Obscurity layers to protect asset information.

Leaks through obscurity layers might make their way through each layer or might be countered by one or more layers. For example, in Figure 7.6, an information leak that would not be countered by any layer might involve someone exercising poor discretion by ignoring data markings (through the first layer), violating information sharing policies (through the second layer), and being ignorant of policies for disclosure after an incident (through the third layer). This demonstrates the human element in the use of discretion to protect critical infrastructure information. Additional examples of obscurity layers in national infrastructure protection include the following:

> Even with layered obscurity, asset information may leak through to an adversary.

- *Public speaking*—A policy might be in place that would deliberately prevent anyone with responsibility for national infrastructure from speaking publicly without explicit public relations preparation and planning.
- *Approved external site*—A ubiquitous mechanism, such as a website, might be in place to constantly and consistently provide organizationally approved information about infrastructure that might be desired by external entities.
- *Search for leakage*—Search engines might be used via ethical hacking techniques to determine the degree and scope of inappropriate information that might already be located on websites or in a cache. This can be complemented by modern data leakage protection (DLP) tools.

As suggested above, the purpose of these discretionary controls is not to suppress information for the purposes of hiding incompetence or inappropriate behavior. The purpose is to responsibly control the type of information made available to a malicious adversary.

Organizational Compartments

An information protection technique used successfully by the U.S. federal government, especially in the military and intelligence communities, involves the compartmentalization of individuals and information. These compartments can be thought of as groups for which some set of policy rules uniformly apply. Typically, individuals are put through a background check to determine their level of trustworthiness. They are then given a designated security *clearance*. Information is similarly put through an analysis to determine its level of criticality; it is then given a designated security *classification*.

> Government clearance levels and information classification are techniques used to protect data by limiting accessibility.

The specifics of how clearances and classifications work are beyond the scope of this book, but a key notion is that each

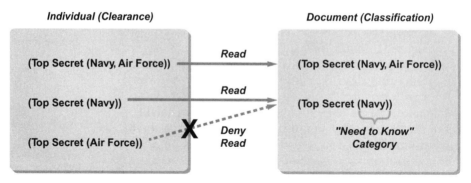

Figure 7.7 Using clearances and classifications to control information disclosure.

combines some notion of hierarchical level (e.g., Top Secret, Secret, Confidential, Unclassified) with a corresponding notion of "need to know" categories (e.g., Navy, Air Force). The cross-product of some set of classified information with the corresponding individuals cleared to access that information is called a *compartment*. Policy rules for accessing data, such as classified documents, from a compartment can then be implemented (see Figure 7.7).

The examples in Figure 7.7 show an individual cleared to Top Secret in categories Navy and Air Force being successful in reading a document that is classified to the same level and categories. In addition, an individual cleared to Top Secret in category Navy is successful reading a document cleared to the same level and categories. On the other hand, an individual cleared to Top Secret in category Air Force is denied access to a document whose category is only Navy. This type of approach is especially powerful in an actual government setting, because information leaks can be interpreted as violations of federal law. In the most intense case, such violations could be interpreted as espionage, with all the associated punishment that comes with such action. The result is a mature environment in most government settings for reducing the chances that national security-related information will be leaked.

Clearly, the protection of national services is not just the responsibility of government. Thus, industry needs a corresponding approach to policy-based access control. The good news is that translation of government compartments to a corporate setting is relatively straightforward. Clearance and classification levels can be mapped to company-defined organizational levels such as "supervisor" and "senior manager." Categories can be mapped to specific projects in a company. Thus, a compartment in some company might correspond to the senior manager level, within some project A and project B (see Figure 7.8).

> Certain secure government data can only be accessed by a few top-level officials.

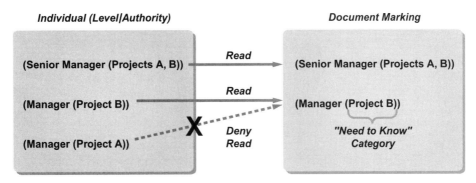

Figure 7.8 Example commercial mapping of clearances and classifications.

The bottom line with compartmentalization is that it should be used to help define boundaries around which information can or cannot be accessed. This helps guide decisions that require human discretion. Too often, in computer security settings today, the underlying goal of many projects and in the management of many critical systems is to avoid the use of information boundaries, often in the interest of openness and sharing. These concepts are valuable for many types of standards, information, data, software, and services, but unfortunately openness and sharing are not always consistent with protecting security-related information about national infrastructure.

> Private companies can mirror government clearance levels by classifying data and limiting access.

National Discretion Program

To implement a national program of information obscurity and discretion, several management and security engineering tasks will be required:

- *TCB definition*—Although it could be difficult to do so, effort should be directed by suitable national authorities toward trying to define a nationwide trusted computing base. This will require coordination between government and industry, but the resulting construct will help direct security management decisions.
- *Reduced emphasis on information sharing*—Government must immediately reduce its emphasis on demanding that information be shared by industry. Any information sharing initiatives that do maintain such an emphasis should focus only on providing government with situation status.
- *Coexistence with hacking community*—The national infrastructure community in government and industry would benefit by creating an improved spirit of cooperation with

the hacking industry. This could come in the form of financial support from government for hacking groups and forums, or it could be more explicit in terms of actual tasking on real programs.

- *Obscurity layered model*—A national obscurity layer should also be put in place to guide decisions about human discretion in protecting sensitive national infrastructure-related information.
- *Commercial information protection models*—Industry should be provided with incentives and rewards for demonstrating some degree of embedded policy-based access control similar to the military model.

Certainly, to increase the chances that these tasks are successful, a culture of human discretion around sensitive information must be created. Senior managers must reinforce this culture by not exercising their right to bypass discretionary controls; for example, all documents, even those created by senior managers, should be marked appropriately. Similarly, if violations of basic information discretion do occur, the consequences should be similarly applied, regardless of organizational position or level.

COLLECTION

*It is important to have a fairly clear understanding of what you
are looking for and what events you are interested in, because you
cannot collect or detect everything.*

Stephen Northcutt[1]

A basic tenet of computer security is that diligent and ongoing
observation of computing and networking behavior can highlight malicious activity. This works best when the observer has
a good frame of reference for what constitutes normal behavior.
Algorithms and human judgment can then be used to compare
profiles with observations to identify activity that might be suspicious. Follow-up analysis can then be used to partition suspicious activity into benign and malicious categories. All this
processing and analysis can only be done in the context of an
existing program of *data collection*.

At the national level, security-relevant data must first be collected at the local or regional level by individual asset managers and a subset then selected for broader aggregation into a
national collection system. In some cases, local and regional collection can be directly connected to national programs. Larger-
scale collection points on wide-area networks, perhaps run by
carriers or government agencies, can also be embedded into the
collection scheme and combined with local, regional, and aggregated data (see Figure 8.1).

Such a national collection process does not exist today in any
organized manner. To build one will require considerable resolve.
From a technical perspective, each collection point requires that
decisions be made about which data is gathered, what methods
will be used for collection, how it will be used, and how it will
be protected. It is not reasonable for any organization to collect
any sort of data without having specific answers to these simple
questions. Improper collection of data, where no clear justification exists for its aggregation, could lead to serious legal, policy,

> Data collection should
> not be attempted until an
> organized plan is in place
> to analyze and protect the
> data.

[1] S. Northcutt, *Network Intrusion Detection: An Analyst's Handbook*, New Riders
Publishing, Berkeley, CA, 1999, p. 34.

Cyber Attacks. DOI: 10.1016/B978-0-12-384917-5.00008-1

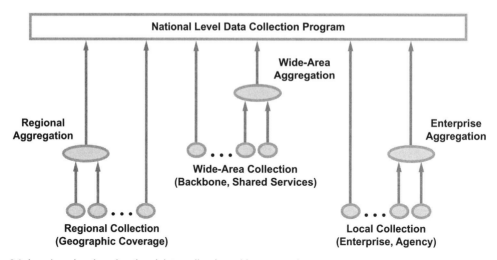

Figure 8.1 Local, regional, and national data collection with aggregation.

or even operational problems for organizations charged with protecting some national asset.

As an illustration, many government groups have done a terrible job in the past protecting data once it has been aggregated. Several years ago, for example, sensitive information collected from chemical companies in the New York area was published by a government agency on its website. This information was then collected by reporters and reproduced as an article in a New York City newspaper, replete with a map showing which types of dangerous chemicals were present and their exact location, as well as noting the health and safety implications of these chemicals. This type of information is of great interest, obviously, to terrorists. Dissemination of this information could also have a negative impact on business operations and the reputations of these companies.

At both local and national levels, data collection decisions for national infrastructure should be based on the following three security goals:

- *Preventing an attack*—Will the data collected help stop a present or future attack? This implies that the recipient of collected data must justify its role in stopping the attack. If the recipient manages some critical infrastructure component, such as a backbone network, that can be used to throttle or stop the attack, then the justification is obvious. If, however, the recipient is a government agency, then the justification might be more difficult.

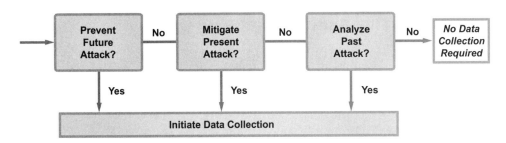

Figure 8.2 Justification-based decision analysis template for data collection.

- *Mitigating an attack*—Will the data collected assist in the response to an ongoing attack? The implication here is that the recipient of data should be able to help interpret what is happening or should be able to direct resources toward a solution. One of the most relevant questions to be answered about an ongoing attack, for example, is how widespread the attack might be. Collecting information from a broad distribution will help to answer this question.
- *Analyzing an attack*—Will the data collected assist in the forensic analysis of an attack after it has occurred? This goal is important but can be easily abused, because it could justify collection of any sort of data available. Forensic analysts generally maintain that their task is made easier in the presence of large volumes of data. Care must therefore be taken to ensure that inappropriate data collection does not occur simply because a forensic analyst might claim to need the information.

These three requirements should direct the scope, coverage, and degree of detail associated with a data collection program for every national infrastructure component. In fact, they provide a suitable template for determining exactly what sort of data should be collected and aggregated. At the local, regional, wide area, and national levels, data collection should only proceed if affirmative answers to these questions can be made (see Figure 8.2).

The decision to *not* collect data might be among the most difficult for any organization, especially a government agency. One of the great axioms of government computer security has been that more data is always better, especially if a path exists to perform such collection. The reality, however, is that improper data collection not only is unnecessary but could also actually weaken national infrastructure.

> Data collection must be justified as to who is collecting the data and why.

> Beware the "more is better" axiom regarding data collection; focus on quality, not quantity.

Collecting Network Data

Perhaps the most useful type of data for collection in national infrastructure is network *metadata*. Also referred to as *netflow*, metadata provides many security-relevant details about network activity. In a Transmission Control Protocol (TCP)/Internet Protocol (IP) environment, metadata allows the security analyst to identify source address, destination address, source port, destination port, protocol, and various header flags in a given session. This information is security relevant because it provides a basis for analyzing activity. A nontechnical analogy would be that metadata is akin to the information that postal workers can see in the mail they process. The size, weight, color, texture, and addressing information on the envelopes and wrappers are apparent, whereas the contents are not.

> Metadata is information *about* the data, not what the data is about.

The collection of metadata involves the placement of equipment or software into the target network for the purpose of producing metadata records. These records are collected and stored for analysis. Obviously, to make this collection feasible, certain functional considerations must be made. There must be legal justification for collecting the data, there must be sufficient storage capacity for maintaining collecting data, and there must be analysts with proper capability to make effective interpretations about the data. Perhaps the most important consideration, however, is whether the collection functionality is sufficiently powerful to keep up with the target network bandwidth capacity (see Figure 8.3).

One issue with large-scale versions of this collection approach is that many metadata collection systems were deployed in carrier backbones during the early part of the century, with the intention of pulling security data from 10-Gbps backbones.

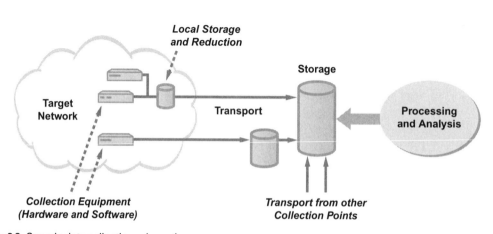

Figure 8.3 Generic data collection schematic.

The challenge is that carrier backbones have begun to grow to 40- and even 100-Gbps capacities. If the collection systems are not increased at a commensurate rate, then the ability to collect metadata could decrease by as much as a factor of ten.

One solution many security analysts use to deal with increasing network capacity is to *sample* the data. This technique involves grabbing some of the data at predetermined intervals so the inbound flow matches the ability to process. Sampled data is generally acceptable for broad analysis of network activity, but it is not as effective for detailed forensics as unsampled metadata. In an unsampled environment, analysts can often detect tiny anomalies in massive amounts of data. This design consideration affects the overall collection process.

As an example, several years ago unsampled metadata on an IP backbone allowed analysts in a global carrier environment to detect that a small number of packets of an unusual protocol type were beginning to show up. Packets of this type had not been seen on the backbone for years, so this was clearly an anomaly to be investigated. Suspicious packets from this unusual event were collected and observed for four days, until a key equipment vendor contacted the carrier to report a serious security flaw in their operating system software. Interestingly, exploits of this vulnerability involved traffic being sent over precisely the protocol type being observed. The collection point thus detected network activity evidence of a security issue that had not even been publicly reported (see Figure 8.4).

> Data collection systems need to keep pace with growth of carrier backbones.

> Sampling data is less time consuming, yet unsampled data may reveal more vulnerabilities in the system.

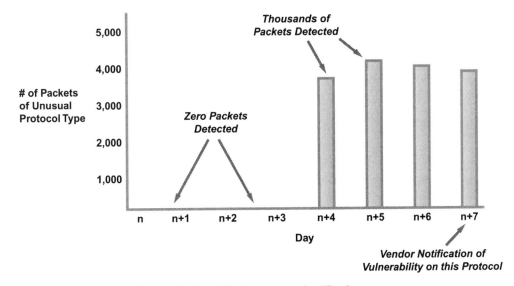

Figure 8.4 Collection detects evidence of vulnerability in advance of notification.

The key observation here is that, under normal conditions, no instances of this type of protocol packet were observed on the carrier backbone. When suddenly the unusual protocol type essentially came alive, there was no easy way to determine why this was the case other than that some sort of anomaly was taking place. When the vendor reported the problem on this protocol, analysts were able to put together this information to solve the riddle of why this anomaly had occurred. This illustrates the importance of integrating all-source information into any data collection environment. National infrastructure protection must include this type of collection and associated analysis to be fully effective in protecting essential services.

> Analysis of unsampled metadata can reveal concerning data traffic patterns that would otherwise go unnoticed.

Collecting System Data

National infrastructure protection initiatives have not traditionally included provision for collecting data from mainframes, servers, and PCs. The justification for such omission is usually based on the scaling and sizing issues inherent in the massive amount of data that would have to be processed from these computers, along with the common view that such systems probably do not provide much security-relevant data. An additional consideration is the potential for privacy abuses, an issue that the citizens of most nations have come to recognize as being important to their lives. As a result, no serious national infrastructure protection initiative to date has included a proposal or plan for this type of functionality.

Regarding scaling and sizing issues, the computing infrastructure required for collection of data from every mainframe, server, and PC deemed part of national infrastructure services would certainly be complex. That said, computing historians know that it is not unprecedented for the complex requirements of one generation to become routine features in another. Furthermore, the tactical approach of identifying a workable subset of the relevant computers in a nation is possible. For example, the mainframes, servers, and PCs running in companies and agencies charged with national infrastructure could be targeted for collection, and this is a tractably sized challenge.

> We may not currently have the capacity to collect data from all relevant computers, but it is an important goal to try to reach.

On the issue of whether mainframes, servers, and PCs provide suitable security-relevant information for national infrastructure protection, many critical incidents are best identified through collection of data at this level. Operating system logs, mainframe event summaries, and PC history records provide excellent evidence that malicious activity might be ongoing. Engineering metrics such as memory utilization or processor load can also provide valuable signals about security issues. For example, when a server shows increases in processor usage as a result of an attack, this condition is often easiest to identify using monitoring tools embedded in the operating system of the computer.

System monitoring is important to national infrastructure protection because it is often the *only* indicator that some security event is under way—even in the presence of firewalls, intrusion detection systems, and other security tools. As a result, national infrastructure protection initiatives will have to include provision for the gathering and processing of data from mainframes, servers, and PCs. This data will have to be selected, collected, transmitted with suitable protection, stored in an environment properly sized for large amounts of data, and processed in real time. Four specific types of information that should be collected include those listed in the box below.

System monitoring provides an overview of activity that may reveal troubling patterns.

Top Four Data Collection Areas

1. *Utilization*—One of the most important metrics in determining whether an attack is ongoing is the utilization profile of servers in the local environment. National asset managers must identify which servers are relevant for monitoring and should instrument an associated program of data collection. This will require cooperation between government and industry, as well as the inclusion of appropriate functional requirements in infrastructure support contracts.

2. *Usage*—Patterns of usage on the mainframes, servers, and PCs in a given nation are important to establish for protection of infrastructure. If certain mainframes are never touched after hours, for example, then this will help to identify smaller attacks during unusual times. Detecting small, active usage events is often easier in a quiet environment than in a noisy environment; however, detecting usage drops is often easier in a noisy environment than in a quieter one.

3. *Applications*—Collecting data about the applications resident on system infrastructure provides useful hints about possible cyber attacks. A common metric is a "top ten" list of most commonly used applications. If the mix changes in some meaningful way, then this could signal an attack. Network gateway systems including proxies are excellent candidates for collecting this type of data for an enterprise. Carriers could provide this type of data in a wide area network or across a given region.

4. *Outages*—Information about outages is important for security, because events that are presumed to have been benign might actually be part of a cyber attack. It is not uncommon for system managers to ignore this possibility; hence, data collection around outages is important. As an example, root-cause analyses after serious outages should be viewed as important information for gathering and analysis.

Two techniques are useful at embedding system management data into cyber security infrastructure. First, an inventory process is required to identify the systems that are considered critical in a given environment. This process might require engineering analysis across relevant government and industrial infrastructure to determine if a given system resides in the critical path of some national service. Alternatively, the decision might be made to try to collect information from every system that is available for collection. Second, for those systems deemed worthy of data collection, a process of either instrumenting or reusing data collection facilities must be identified. This could involve the use of operating system audit trails or it could involve the installation of some sort of application-level logging program.

Regardless of the approach, data would flow from the target computers of interest across some network medium to various aggregation points. Regional and enterprise networks would probably have to introduce an aggregation function for their organization before the data is shared externally. One would expect that network carriers could easily step into this role of providing different types of aggregations; that is, customers of DSL and cable services could agree, under suitable incentives, to allow for collection of data related to the presence of malware, viruses, and other compromising software. Encryption could be used to help protect the confidentiality of the data in transit and storage.

> Aggregation points would allow for regional collection of data.

There would also have to be some sort of filtering or data reduction to focus the collection on specific systems of interest and to limit data to only that which is likely to be useful. For example, if a nation tried to collect security-related data from hundreds of thousands or millions of PCs every day, the resultant daily dataflow would be measured in the multiple terabyte range. Commercial databases would probably be insufficient for storing this volume, so customized databases would be required. The volume of collected data would ultimately be made available to a security processing and interpretive system that could be used for national infrastructure purposes.

Although more creative overall architectures could be imagined, such as peer-to-peer, the centralized collection approach would be more likely to be implemented in practice. It also lends itself quite well to the establishment and operation of a national security operations center (see Figure 8.5).

Readers might cringe at the idea of collecting data in this manner, especially from end-user PCs scattered across a nation, but this practice is more common than one might think. Every large enterprise and government agency, for example, routinely embeds integrity management software, such as tripwire functionality, into their mainframes and servers. Furthermore, almost every enterprise and agency uses software agents on PCs to collect relevant security and management data. Perhaps ironically,

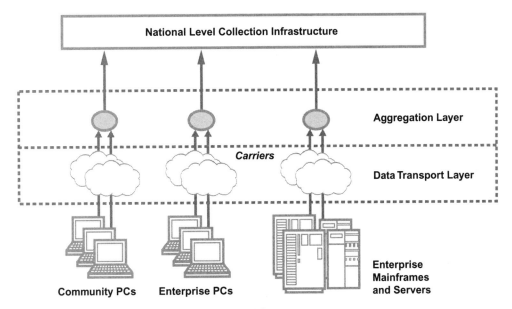

Figure 8.5 Collecting data from mainframes, servers, and PCs.

botnet operators have also perfected the idea of collecting data from massive numbers of end-user computers for the purpose of attack. The idea that this general schema would be extended to benevolent national infrastructure protection seems straightforward.

> A national data collection center may not differ much from current enterprise and agency data collection.

The challenge is that this sort of scheme can be abused. Computer scientists lament software running with high privilege on their systems, and citizens resist the notion of an unknown monitor pulling data from their system to some unknown collection facility, possibly violating privacy principles. Both concerns are valid and need to be debated publicly. If an acceptable compromise is reached between government and its businesses and citizenry, then the result can be incorporated into the design of an appropriate national system. At minimum, such a compromise would have to include demonstrable evidence that mainframes, servers, and PCs provide only harmless computer security-related information such as scan data, security state, and signature-based malware detection. Anything more penetrating that might allow, for example, remote access and execution from a centralized control station would probably be unacceptable, even though organizations do this routinely with their employee base.

> A national data collection program would have to be sensitive to citizens' concerns for privacy.

Another possibility might be some sort of citizen-sponsored, citizen-run, grassroots data collection effort for PCs and servers, where participants agree to provide security information to a massive distributed system of peers. Such a system would not perfectly match the geographic or political perimeter of a nation, and many citizens would refuse to participate based on principle. Few members, however, of massive peer-to-peer networks for music or video complain about the privacy implications of running such software, often questionable or illegal, on their local machine. They just enjoy getting free content. The idea that a similar construct could be used to help secure national infrastructure would require demonstrating some sort of benefit to participants. This may not be possible, but the effort is worthwhile from a security perspective because data collected from a massive deployment of computers across a given nation would provide a valuable and unmatched window into the security posture of national infrastructure.

> Citizens who see the benefit of a national data collection system would likely be willing to participate voluntarily.

Security Information and Event Management

The process of aggregating system data from multiple sources for the purposes of protection is referred to in the computer security community as *security information and event management* (SIEM). Today, SIEM tools can be purchased that allow collection of a diverse set of technologies from different vendors. This typically includes firewalls, intrusion detection systems (IDS), servers, routers, and applications. Just about every commercial enterprise and government agency today includes some sort of SIEM deployment. One could easily imagine this functionality being extended to include collection feeds from mainframes, servers, and PCs (see Figure 8.6).

The SIEM system will include translation functions to take proprietary outputs, logs, and alarm streams from the different vendors into a common format. From this common collection format, a set of common functions can thus be performed, including data storage, display, sharing, and analysis. National infrastructure protection must include rational means for interpreting SIEM data from components, if only because many organizations will already have a SIEM system in place for processing their locally collected data. This interpretation of SIEM data from multiple feeds will be complicated by the fact that most existing SIEM deployments in different companies, sectors, and government agencies are mutually compatible. A more critical problem, however, is the reluctance among most security managers to instrument a real-time connection from their SIEM system to a national collection system. A comparable problem is that service

> Security managers will be reluctant to link their SIEM system to a national collection system.

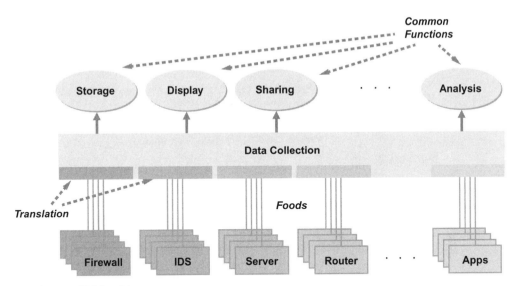

Figure 8.6 Generic SIEM architecture.

providers do not currently feed the output of their consumer customers' data into a regional SIEM system.

In any event, the architecture for a national system of data collection using SIEM functionality is not hard to imagine. Functionally, each SIEM system could be set up to collect, filter, and process locally collected data for what would be considered nationally relevant data for sharing. This filtered data could then be sent encrypted over a network to an aggregation point, which would have its own SIEM functionality. Ultimately, SIEM functions would reside at the national level for processing data from regional and enterprise aggregation points. In this type of architecture, local SIEM systems can be viewed as data sources, much as the firewalls, intrusion detection systems, and the like are viewed in a local SIEM environment (see Figure 8.7).

> Local and regional SIEM systems would work as filters to feed only relevant data to a national collection point.

Unfortunately, most local infrastructure managers have not been comfortable with the architecture shown in Figure 8.7 for several reasons. First, there are obviously costs involved in setting up this sort of architecture, and generally these funds have not been made available by government groups. Second, it is possible that embedded SIEM functionality could introduce functional problems in the local environment. It can increase processor utilization on systems with embedded SIEM hooks, and it can clog up network environments, especially gateway choke points, with data that might emanate from the collection probes.

> Will a national data collection system put an increased financial burden on private agencies and enterprises?

A much more critical problem with the idea of national SIEM deployment is that most enterprise and government agency

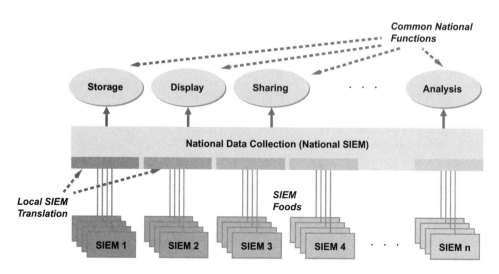

Figure 8.7 Generic national SIEM architecture.

security managers will never be comfortable with their sensitive security data leaving local enterprise premises. Certainly, a managed security service provider might be already accepting and processing security data in a remote location, but this is a virtual private arrangement between a business and its supplier. The data is not intended for analysis other than to directly benefit the originating environment. Furthermore, a service level agreement generally dictates the terms of the engagement and can be terminated by the enterprise or agency at any time. No good solutions exist for national SIEM implementation, other than the generally agreed-upon view that national collection leads to better national security, which in turn benefits everyone.

> There are still too many unanswered questions about the security of sensitive data leaving private enterprises.

Large-Scale Trending

The most fundamental processing technique used for data that is collected across national infrastructure involves the identification of *trends*. In many cases, trends in collected data are obvious, as in simple aggregate volume increases, such as packets delivered on a network. In other cases, however, trends might not be so obvious. For instance, when the collection process or monitored systems are experiencing change, the trend identification might not be easy. Suppose, for example, that a monitored network is growing, but the collection system is not. The result is that critical data might be missed, which could be misleading.

Similarly, if a change is made to the underlying collection system, perhaps involving a new technology or vendor, then this could influence the trends presumably being observed.

At the simplest level, a trend involves some quantitative attribute going up (growth), going down (reduction), staying the same (leveling), or doing none of the above (unpredictability). When data jumps around, for example, it might not be easy to draw a conclusion; however, the fact that it is jumping around might itself be an important and useful conclusion. Perhaps the most common question infrastructure managers ask with respect to security is whether attacks are increasing, decreasing, or staying the same with respect to some component in question. This question about attack trends is a favorite among CEOs and national legislators. It can only be answered accurately in the context of collected data.

> Tracking trends may tell us whether adversarial attacks are increasing, decreasing, or staying the same.

As a concrete example, over a nine-month period from June 2006 to March 2007, a stable collection system embedded in a global service provider's backbone detected an increase in behavior consistent with malicious bots. As was outlined in the first chapter, a bot is a piece of software inserted into a target system, usually a broadband-connected PC, for malicious or questionable purposes. The bot might be used to attack some target, it might be used to send spam, or it might be used to steal personal information. The detection of bot behavior comes from collecting traffic information for the purpose of identifying communication between a number of end-user PCs and a smaller number of servers on the Internet.

By collecting evidence of bot behavior and rendering the results in a simple histogram, the growth of bots can be seen clearly, and local management decisions can be made accordingly (see Figure 8.8).

Most managers shown the growth trend in Figure 8.8 would conclude that bots represented an increasing threat during this time period; however, proper national infrastructure protection requires a more thorough analysis before any real conclusions are drawn. The following are some basic practical considerations that must be made by security analysts before the trend in any data collection chart can be trusted:

> Collected data must be analyzed to determine what it can accurately tell us about trends.

- *Underlying collection*—Amazingly, trend data such as that shown in Figure 8.8 is often provided in the context of a collection architecture that might be changing. For example, if a collection system for bots is getting more accurate through algorithmic improvements or better coverage, then the observed growth in bots might simply reflect a more effective use of detection tools.

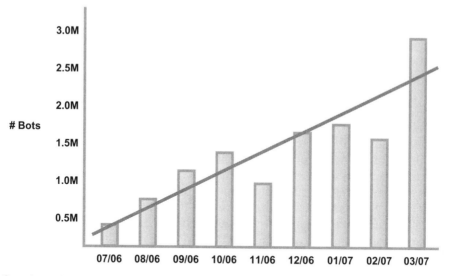

Figure 8.8 Growth trend in botnet behavior over 9-month period (2006–2007).

- *Volunteered data*—It is common for government organizations to use data volunteered from commercial entities as the basis for drawing conclusions about trends. This can be dangerous, because weak or nonexistent controls are in place regarding how the information is collected and managed. It is also possible that data might be volunteered that is incorrect or tampered with for some malicious or mischievous purpose.
- *Relevant coverage*—The amount of coverage across the environment in which the data is collected will affect the validity of an observed trend. Suppose, for example, that a small organization with an Internet connection uses that connection to draw conclusions about traffic trends. This certainly would be a less attractive vantage point than a global Internet carrier making the same determination.

These issues highlight the importance of national infrastructure managers taking a mature approach to the interpretation of collected data. This is especially important because trend information so often drives the allocation of critical resources and funding. At the national level, for example, experienced security experts can point to dozens of cases where some sort of trend is used to advance the case for the funding of an initiative. This often involves hype about the rise of some virus or worm.

The Conficker worm, for example, reportedly included some sort of embedded attack that would occur on April 1, 2009. Conficker

> Trends must be interpreted carefully before they are used to justify changes in funding levels.

was especially relevant—and still is—because its operation involved several million bots. This makes it one of the more potentially powerful botnets known to the security community. Most security experts understood that there was nothing in the Conficker code to suggest such an event on that particular date, but predicted attack dates are convenient for attracting attention and are thus common. National infrastructure protection begs a more mature approach to the public interpretation of collected data.

Tracking a Worm

Data collection provides an excellent means for tracking a worm. Recall that a worm is a program that does three things: (1) it finds network-visible computers that can accept a copy of the worm program, (2) it sends a copy of itself to one of the identified network-visible machines, and (3) it initiates remote execution of the new remote instance of the program on the network-visible target. This starts a chain reaction in which the identifying, copying, and remote execution continue indefinitely. By collecting network metadata while this is all happening, security analysts can generally determine what the worm is doing and how serious the event might be. In the best possible cases, the collection might even provide hints that can be used to stop a worm from developing, which is obviously attractive for national infrastructure security.

> Collecting network metadata allows security analysts to track a worm's progress and predict its course.

In 2003 and 2004, the Internet experienced an unusually large number of worm events. This was due primarily to the poor processes that were in place at the time for operating system and application-level software patching. This patching problem was true for both enterprise systems and home broadband users. During this time period, one worm after another seemed to rage across the Internet, and most observers viewed these events as largely spontaneous; that is, the general consensus was that worms would spread in just a few minutes, and that data collection was useless. If a worm was going to get you, the thinking went, it would get you fast, and there was nothing you could do in advance to stop the event.

The reality of the situation was actually more subtle. The SQL/Slammer worm of January 2003, for example, was one that appeared to have a spontaneous impact on traffic. In the minutes during which the worm appeared to have spread significantly, packets of User Datagram Protocol (UDP) traffic went from small, predictable volumes with few anomalies to an immediately spiked upward volume. On first glance, this happened in a

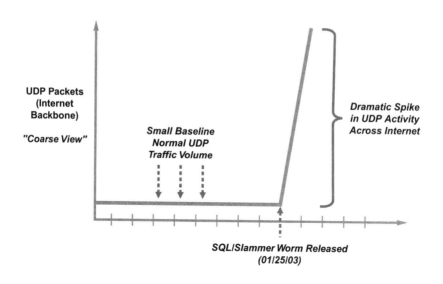

Figure 8.9 Coarse view of UDP traffic spike from SQL/Slammer worm. (Figure courtesy of Dave Gross and Brian Rexroad.)

manner that suggested no warnings, no time for preparation, and no time for incident response (see Figure 8.9).

The spike in packet volume due to the SQL/Slammer worm certainly appeared to be immediate and without warning. Upon much closer examination, however, one finds that the UDP data leading up to this event might have carried some indications and warning value from a security perspective. In particular, starting in early January 2003, UDP volumes on the specific SQL port used by the worm were displaying anomalous behavior. On January 2, 2003, the first spike occurred, and this was followed by three weeks of similarly odd behavior. While it might be a stretch to absolutely conclude that these odd spikes were early attempts at producing a worm, no one can argue that they suggested a serious change in UDP behavior on the Internet (see Figure 8.10).

The suggestion here is that a more detailed inspection of UDP behavior on the SQL port before the SQL/Slammer worm achieved its aim could have given valuable data to security engineers. In particular, the vulnerability exploited by the SQL/Slammer worm was known at the time, although most security managers were lax to install the patch. If the information in Figure 8.10 had been widely disseminated at the time, then anyone wise enough to heed the warning and install the patch would have been immune from the SQL/Slammer worm. The implications of this situation should be obvious from the perspective of national infrastructure protection.

Collecting and analyzing data are important steps; the next is acting on the data in a timely manner.

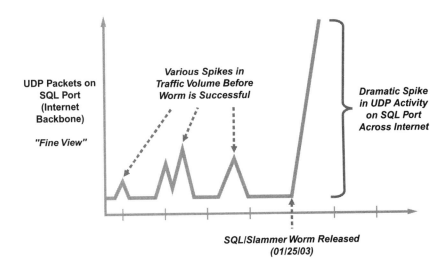

Figure 8.10 Fine view of UDP traffic spike due to SQL/Slammer worm. (Figure courtesy of Dave Gross and Brian Rexroad.)

National Collection Program

Implementing a program of national data collection for infrastructure security will require a combination of public outreach initiatives before any large-scale structures can be put in place. The citizenry and business community must fully understand the purpose, usage, and controls associated with a collection system. Mechanisms for preventing privacy abuses must be paramount in the discussion and embedded into any architecture that might be proposed. The specifics of how this debate might be influenced are beyond the scope of this book, but it goes without saying that no national collection program can be successful without this requisite step.

Once general acceptance has been obtained for the creation of a national data collection program, the following technical and architectural issues must be addressed:

- *Data sources*—National attention is required to define which data sources are deemed valuable for providing security information to the broad collection function. Important mainframes and servers in organizations and agencies charged with infrastructure protection would seem the most obvious to include. End-user PCs owned and operated by private citizens would probably be the most difficult to include.

> A successful national data collection program must address the concerns of citizens and the business community regarding protection of private data.

- *Protected transit*—Security-relevant data collected from identified sources would need to be transmitted via suitable networks with sufficient encryption. Sizing consideration could dictate limits on the amount of information that could be pulled from a particular source.
- *Storage considerations*—The amount of information collected is obviously controllable, but the appetite for data from security analysts is usually unlimited. As such, pressure would exist to maximize the amount of information stored, as well as the length of time the data is available for analysis.
- *Data reduction emphasis*—Across the entire national initiative for data collection, time and energy should be directed toward reducing the amount of data being handled. Obviously, this is critical if a given collection method should inadvertently grab more information than is needed or might include information that has no relevance to the security challenge.

While each of these issues represents a technical challenge, particularly in terms of sizing and scaling, they can be combined into a reasonable system if engineered properly. The overall approach will benefit from stepwise refinement methods that start with a tractable subset of data sources initially which gradually increases with time.

> A planned, stepwise approach to national data collection could create a system that would be of immense value in the quest to protect our national infrastructure.

CORRELATION

A benefit of anomaly detection is that it can potentially recognize unforeseen attacks. A limitation is that it can be hard to distinguish normal from abnormal behavior.

Dorothy Denning[1]

Computer and network security experts understand that correlation is one of the most powerful analytic methods available for threat investigation. Intrusion detection systems, for example, are only useful when the alarm streams that result from signature or profile-based processing can be correlated with data from other areas. When alarms are viewed in isolation, they are of only limited use. This limitation in processing alarms is directly related to the complexity of the target environment; that is, decision makers in more complex environments will be more reliant on correlating collected data than in more limited environments. Proper national infrastructure protection is therefore highly dependent upon a coordinated program of information correlation from all available sources.

Data in a vacuum is irrelevant; it must be compared with other data to determine its relevance and importance.

From a foundational perspective, four distinct analytic methods are available for correlating cyber security information: *profile-based*, *signature-based*, *domain-based*, and *time-based correlation*. Profile-based correlation involves comparison of a normal profile of target activity with observed patterns of activity. Presumably, if a substantive difference exists between normal and observed, this could signal a possible intrusion. Obviously, many situations exist where observed activity is not normal but does not signal an intrusion. Websites running specials or supporting some limited-time engagement, for example, will see traffic spikes during these periods that do not match normal patterns. Nevertheless, anomalies with activity profiles are worthy of attention from a security perspective (see Figure 9.1).

Comparing data determines what is normal and what is an anomaly.

Signature-based correlation involves comparing a signature pattern of some known malicious condition to observed activity. If the two match, then high confidence exists that an intrusion

---

[1] D. Denning, *Information Warfare and Security*, Addison-Wesley, New York, 1999, p. 362.

Cyber Attacks. DOI: 10.1016/B978-0-12-384917-5.00009-3

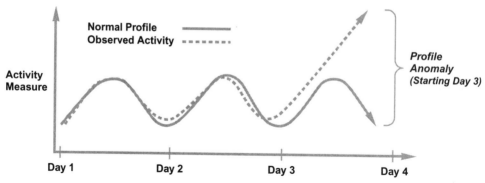

Figure 9.1 Profile-based activity anomaly.

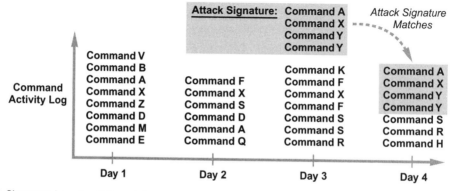

Figure 9.2 Signature-based activity match.

is under way. The challenge is when observed activity shares characteristics with a signature but does not exactly match. This requires diligence from the security team to stay focused. Most signature-based correlation patterns involve some sequence of events, such as commands, which are defined as a discrete signature, and comparison against logs of observed activity. For example, antivirus software, antispam algorithms, and intrusion detection systems all operate in this manner (see Figure 9.2).

Domain-based correlation involves comparing data from one domain with data collected in an entirely different context. Relevant differences in the data collection environments include computing environment, software architecture, networking technology, application profiles, and type of business being supported. For example, data collected by a power company about an attack could easily differ from data collected by a federal civilian agency on the same incident. Similarly, two targets of a botnet attack could report different isolated views that could

> Data comparison, especially from different domains, creates a clearer picture of adversary activity.

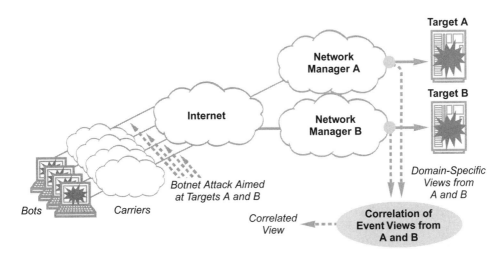

Figure 9.3 Domain-based correlation of a botnet attack at two targets.

be correlated into a single common view. This requires a prearranged transport, collection, and analysis approach leading to a common correlated output (see Figure 9.3).

Time-based correlation compares data collected during one time period with data collected at a different time. This can involve the same or different data source but is obviously more effective if the data source is the same, because this removes one variable from the correlative analysis. Many types of attacks will not be time sensitive and are thus not well suited to this type of correlation; for example, a single break-in, during which malware is embedded in a target system, might not be a good candidate for time-based correlation. Attacks that are multistage, however, such as many "low and slow" approaches, are quite well suited to the approach. Botnet attacks are increasingly being designed by adversaries in this manner, with the distributed program attacking its target in a slower and more deliberate manner than via a single bombardment. Detection of such an event is well suited to time-based correlation, because potentially significant time periods could exist between successive steps in an attack. Time-based correlation would be required to connect relevant steps and to filter out noisy, irrelevant activity (see Figure 9.4).

> Changes that appear over time may indicate a slowly building, deliberate attack.

The essence of correlation in cyber security involves comparison of various pieces of data to determine whether an intrusion is under way. In the most desirable set of circumstances, this involves comparing two pieces of data for which every associated, relevant attribute is the same *except for one*. Such a scenario allows the analyst to focus in on that one attribute. Time-based

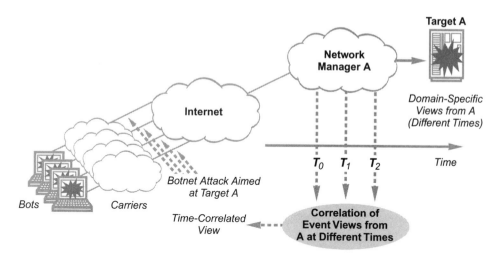

Figure 9.4 Time-based correlation of a botnet attack.

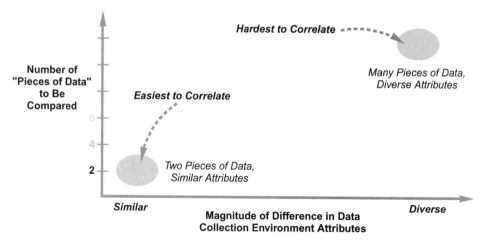

Figure 9.5 Taxonomy of correlation scenarios.

correlation works nicely when the collection environment is exactly the same but the data is collected at different times. The analyst does not have to worry about whether changes in other factors are affecting the data, as only the time changes. In the most complex case, however, multiple pieces of data are collected from environments where the associated, relevant attributes differ. The analyst thus must juggle concerns about which attributes in which environments might be affecting the data. This greatly complicates the correlation task (see Figure 9.5).

This data collection attribute taxonomy is important to national infrastructure, because most practical cases tend to be very complex cases that are difficult to correlate. Information that becomes available during an incident usually originates from wildly different sources with diverse collection methods, processing tools, network views, and so on. Worm events on the Internet, for example, are often observed with considerable scrutiny by some organizations (perhaps with bad consequences), whereas other groups might not even notice that a security event is ongoing. Only the most mature correlation analysts will have the ability to factor these differences in viewpoint into an accurate broad conclusion about security. To date, this has required experienced human beings with considerable training. Additional research is required before dependable tools will be available to perform accurate correlation on multiple, diverse inputs.

> We currently rely on human analysis of data across different domains and during different time periods; no software or program can factor in all relevant elements.

Conventional Security Correlation Methods

The current state of the practice in day-to-day network security correlation in existing national infrastructure settings is based on a technique known as *threat management*. In this approach, data aggregated from multiple sources is correlated to identify patterns, trends, and relationships. The overall approach relies on a *security information and event management* (SIEM) system for the underlying collection and aggregation of relevant data. A SIEM system does the best it can in terms of identifying correlation instances, using the best available algorithms for profile, signature, domain, and time-based analysis, subject to the practical limitations mentioned above. Four of the primary feeds into a typical commercially available SIEM tool for threat management are listed in the box.

Information Feeds for SIEM Threat Management

- *Firewall audit trails*—Firewalls generate audit records when certain types of security-relevant events occur such as denied connection requests. These records are of limited use in isolation but are often useful for correlation with other data. Other static information about a firewall, such as its inbound and outbound policy, is also important for correlation.
- *Intrusion detection and prevention system alarms*—Intrusion detection and prevention systems are designed specifically to generate alarm data when suspicious activity is observed. The problem is that it is not always easy to determine if something suspicious is truly malicious. Generally, correlation with other data is required to make this determination.

- *Operating system or application logs*—Output log files generated by activity on an operating system or software application can provide useful indications and warnings for security. The first step in forensics, for example, involves examination of log files for evidence. (Good hackers know not to leave such obvious tracks, of course.) In addition to logs, the specific attributes of the operating system and application are also important for correlation. This can include version, vendor, and configuration data.
- *Network device metadata*—Information about network behavior is quickly becoming recognized by cyber security experts as possibly being the most powerful tool available for threat management. Metadata showing source and destination information about addresses and ports, as well as information about protocol, direction of flow, and status of protocol flags and settings, gives security analysts a view into network activity unavailable through any other means.

The interplay between the various security devices in a local threat management system is sometimes straightforward. If an intrusion detection system generates an alarm signaling some sort of problem involving a given Internet protocol (IP) source address and corresponding destination port, and if the local environment also allows inbound traffic to this destination port, then the correlation process could generate a recommendation that the local firewall block either this source address or this port. Many commercial firewalls and intrusion detection systems provide this capability today, although the reality is that many network managers do not make use of this type of protection. This is usually due to a lack of familiarity with the process, as well as a common lack of local knowledge about the egress and ingress traffic through an enterprise gateway or perimeter. This is a shame, because when it is done properly the protection achieved can be quite powerful (see Figure 9.6).

> Many security managers underutilize the commercial firewalls at their disposal.

The example shown above demonstrates the natural feedback loop that can occur when data is correlated—that is, as interpretation resulting from the correlation task is fed back to the firewall as a new data input. This in turn affects processing and will eventually change the correlation function output. This feedback loop will cease when the resultant interpretations are no longer new and have no changes to report back to the firewall. Security managers often configure their intrusion detection systems to suppress output when this steady-state condition occurs. This reduces operator burden but great care must be taken to ensure that valid indicators are not being missed.

> Exercise caution in suppressing output once a steady-state condition has been achieved; otherwise, valid indicators may be missed.

The correlation function can extend to different parts of the same organization with different networks, servers, applications, and management groups. Surprisingly, many correlation activities

If two bots can generate 1 Mbps of attack traffic, then a target with a 1-Gbps inbound connection can be filled up by 2000 bots, which turns out to be a modestly sized botnet. Following this logic, a much larger botnet, perhaps with hundreds of thousands or even millions of bots, can be viewed as a particularly substantive problem for national infrastructure that requires attention. The correlation issue in this case is that no single endpoint will have a suitable vantage point to determine the size, scope, or intensity of a given botnet. One might suggest that the only reasonable chance one has of actually performing the proper correlation relative to a botnet is in the context of carrier infrastructure.

Steps for Botnet Detection

The steps involved in the detection of a botnet via correlative analysis by a network carrier are roughly as follows:

1. *Broad data collection*—The detection of a botnet requires a broad enough vantage point for collecting data from both broadband-connected PCs as well as enterprise servers visible to the Internet. The type of information needed is essentially netflow-type metadata, including source, destination, and traffic types.

2. *One-to-many communication correlation*—From the collected data, the correlative analysis must focus on identifying the typical one-to-many fan-out pattern found in a distributed botnet. This pattern can include several botnet controllers, so multiple one-to-many relations typically overlap in a botnet.

3. *Geographic location correlation*—It is helpful to match up the bots and controllers to a geographic location using the associated IP address. This does not provide pinpoint accuracy, but it offers a general sense of where the bots and controllers are located.

4. *Vigilant activity watch*—The security analysis should include close, vigilant watch of activity from the bots and servers. The most important activity to be identified would be a distributed attack from the bots to some target.

The steps in the box above allow for the construction of a logical map of a botnet, showing the geographic locations of the bots, their associated service provider (usually a local broadband carrier), the set of servers used as botnet controllers, and a general depiction of any relevant activity. Typical activity found in a botnet includes recruitment of new bots, as well as attacks from the bots toward some designated target (see Figure 9.9).

Botnets can have a far-reaching geographic distribution.

The botnet diagram demonstrates some of the conclusions that can be drawn immediately from such an analysis. The typical pattern of bot clumping that one finds in a botnet might give hints as to the type of social engineering or lure used to drop malware onto the target PCs. Useful hints might also be gathered from regions where the botnet seems to have gathered no bots.

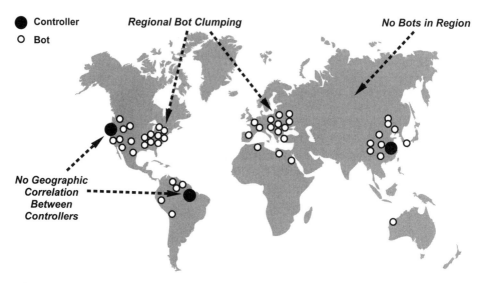

Figure 9.9 Correlative depiction of a typical botnet.

One area where correlative analysis is often not useful is trying to determine correlations between the geographic locations of botnet controllers. This generally results in no useful information, as botnet controllers tend to be scattered across the globe, driven by opportunistic hacking.

It goes without saying that national infrastructure protection requires the real-time capability to monitor botnet configuration and activity. The risk of botnets has grown so much in recent years partly because they have been able to exist under the radar of most government and commercial organizations. The first step in reducing this risk involves the creation of a national capability to collect information about botnets and to advise the participants on how best to avoid being either duped into hacking someone else or directly targeted for an attack.

> Disseminating information about botnet tactics may help consumers avoid future lures.

Large-Scale Correlation Process

For national infrastructure protection, large-scale correlation of all-source data by organizations with a broad vantage point is complicated by several technical, operational, and business factors, including the following:

- *Data formats*—Individual national asset environments will most likely collect data in incompatible formats due to a lack of standards in security data collection tools. As a result,

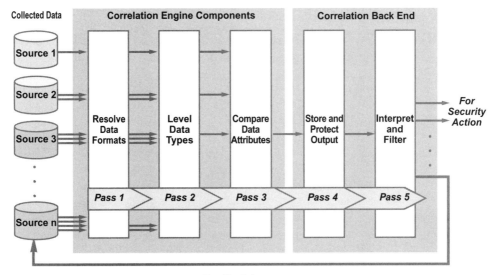

Figure 9.10 Large-scale, multipass correlation process with feedback.

almost all security-relevant data is collected in a proprietary or locally defined format. This represents a significant challenge for any large-scale collection from multiple sources.

- *Collection targets*—Individual asset environments will likely collect data from different types of events and triggers. Some, for example, might collect detailed information about networks and only limited information from systems, whereas others might do the opposite. This obviously complicates the comparison of aggregated data from multiple sources.

- *Competition*—Various commercial groups collecting relevant data might be in direct business competition. (Most government groups will admit to their share of mutual competition as well.) This competitive profile implies that any aggregated information and any interpretation that would result from correlative analysis must be carefully protected and associated with suitable anonymity.

To deal with these challenges on a large scale, a deliberate correlation process must be employed. The process must break down each component of the correlation task into discrete entities with well-defined inputs and outputs. This process is best viewed in aggregate as consisting of five different passes leading from collected data to actionable information (see Figure 9.10).

Large-scale data correlation initiatives must overcome challenges posed by competition, incompatible data formats, and differing collection targets.

Five Passes Leading to Actionable Information

1. The first pass in this process schema involves resolution of all incompatible data formats from the different sources. In addition to the data generated by familiar security devices, these inputs can also include human-generated data that could be obtained through telephony or even social processes. The resolution must be automated via filters that produce a common output. Amazingly, very little work has been done in the computer security community to standardize relevant formats.

2. The second pass in the schema involves a leveling of the various types of data collected. The most common task in this pass is to categorize similar data into the appropriate set of categories. This must be done because different organizations routinely refer to the same security-relevant events by different names. Commercial tools also tend to refer to the same attacks by different names and alarm types. Large-scale correlation thus requires a common understanding of the semantics associated with activity of interest. Small-scale analysis methodologies using a common threat management tool from one vendor can skip this step; large-scale analysis from multiple, diverse sources cannot.

3. The third pass involves the actual comparison of collected data to relevant attributes. Computer security experts often refer to this pass itself as correlation. This pass is where security algorithms for profile, signature, domain, and time-based correlation are incorporated into the analysis. It typically involves a combination of automated processing using tools, with the interpretation of human experts. In the best case, this pass in the process occurs rapidly, almost in real time, but the reality is that the analysis step can take considerable time in the most complex scenarios. This pass, along with the first two passes, can be viewed collectively as the *correlation engine*.

4. The fourth pass involves storage and protection of the output. This is likely to include interpretation of the data once it has been aggregated and compared. Insights are often evident at this stage of the process, and these can be represented as either deliberately stored information in a database or simply as information known to security analysts involved in the overall process. In either case, the information must be protected. For large-scale applications, the size of the information collected can be massive, which implies that special database technology with the ability to scale might be required.

5. The fifth and last pass in the process involves filtering and dissemination of the information. This might result in a feedback loop where output recommendations become input to a new series of five correlation passes. Alternatively, it can be used by appropriate parties for immediate action such as real-time incident response. This pass, along with the storage pass, can be viewed collectively as the *correlation back end*.

National Correlation Program

Data collection can be encouraged by making it a requirement of contracted government-related projects.

Implementation of a national correlation program is likely to follow two specific directions. First, steps might be taken to encourage individual organizations with national infrastructure responsibility to create and follow a local program of data correlation. This can be done by embedding correlation requirements into standard audit and certification standards, as well as within any program solicitations for government-related infrastructure work. The likelihood of success of this approach is high and is thus recommended for immediate adoption at the national policy level.

Second, national-level programs might be created to try to correlate collected data at the highest level from all available sources. This approach is much more challenging and requires addressing the following technical and operational issues:

- *Transparent operations*—The analysis approach used for correlation should be fully known to all participants. Thus, whether profiles, signatures, or the like are used, the process should be clearly explained and demonstrated. This will allow participants to help improve such aspects of the process as data feed provision, data reduction algorithms, and back-end interpretation.
- *Guaranteed data feeds*—Any participant providing data to the correlation process must be held to a guaranteed service level. Obviously, this level can change but only under controlled conditions that can be factored into the analysis. Without such guarantees, correlation algorithms will not work.
- *Clearly defined value proposition*—Participants should recognize a clearly defined value proposition for their provision of data. The worst situation involves a "black hole" collection process where the output recommendations from the correlation activity are not generally shared.
- *Focus on situational awareness*—The output of the process should certainly be action oriented but should also recognize the limitations inherent in broad correlation. It is unlikely that any national-level correlation function will be able to give a real-time silver bullet to any participant. More likely, the output will provide situational awareness that will help in the interpretation or response to an event.

By addressing these issues, the technical and operational feasibility of a successful, national-level correlation function increases dramatically. Unfortunately, many legal, social, and political issues—considered outside the general scope of this book—will complicate the creation of such a function.

AWARENESS

Intelligence, the information and knowledge about an adversary obtained through observation, investigation, analysis, or understanding, is the product that provides battlespace awareness.

Edward Waltz[1]

Situational awareness refers to the collective real-time understanding within an organization of its security risk posture. Security risk measures the likelihood that an attack might produce significant consequences to some set of locally valued assets. A major challenge is that the factors affecting security risk are often not locally controlled and are often deliberately obscured by an adversary. To optimize situation awareness, considerable time, effort, and even creativity must be expended. Sadly, most existing companies and agencies with responsibility for national infrastructure have little or no discipline in this area. This is surprising, as a common question asked by senior leadership is whether the organization is experiencing a security risk or is "under attack" at a given time.

Awareness of security posture requires consideration of several technical, operational, business, and external or global factors. These include the following:

- *Known vulnerabilities*—Detailed knowledge of relevant vulnerabilities from vendors, service providers, government, academia, and the hacking community is essential to effective situational awareness. Specific events such as prominent hacking conferences are often a rich source of new vulnerability data.

> Consider attending a hacking conference to learn more about potential vulnerabilities.

- *Security infrastructure*—Understanding the state of all active security components in the local environment is required for proper situational awareness. This includes knowledge of security software versions for integrity management and anti-malware processing, signature deployments for security devices such as intrusion detection systems, and monitoring

[1] E. Waltz, *Information Warfare: Principles and Operations*, Artech House, Norwood, MA, 1998.

Cyber Attacks. DOI: 10.1016/B978-0-12-384917-5.00010-X

status for any types of security collection and processing systems.

- *Network and computing architecture*—Knowledge of network and computing architecture is also important to understanding an organization's situational security posture. An accurate catalog of all inbound and outbound services through external gateways is particularly important during an incident that might be exploiting specific ports or protocols.

- *Business environment*—Security posture is directly related to business activities such as new product launches, new project initiation, public relations press releases, executive action involving anything even mildly controversial, and especially any business failures. Any types of contract negotiations between management and employee bases have a direct impact on the local situational security status.

- *Global threats*—Any political or global threats that might be present at a given time will certainly have an impact on an organization's situational security posture. This must be monitored carefully in regions where an organization might have created a partnership or outsourcing arrangement. Because outsourcing tends to occur in regions that are remote to the organization, a global threat posture has become more significant.

- *Hardware and software profiles*—An accurate view of all hardware and software currently in place in the organization is also essential to situational awareness. A common problem involves running some product version that is too old to properly secure through a program of patching or security enhancement. A corresponding problem involves systems that are too new to properly characterize their robustness against attack. In practice, an optimal period of product operation emerges between the earliest installation period, when a product or system is brand new, and the latter stages of deployment, when formal support from a vendor might have lapsed (see Figure 10.1).

Each of these factors presents a set of unique challenges for security teams. An emerging global conflict, for example, will probably have nothing to do with the vulnerability profile of software running locally in an enterprise. There are, however, clear dependencies that arise between factors in practice and will improve situational awareness. For example, when vulnerabilities are reported by a hacking group, the organization's security posture will depend on its local hardware, software, and security infrastructure profile. As a result, it is generally reasonable for an organization to combine the value of all situational status factors

The increase in global outsourcing requires awareness of how international political events may impact your vendors.

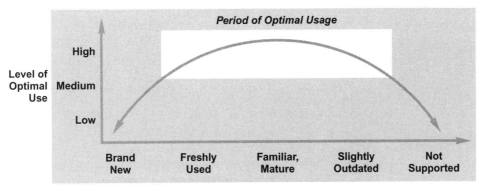

Figure 10.1 Optimal period of system usage for cyber security.

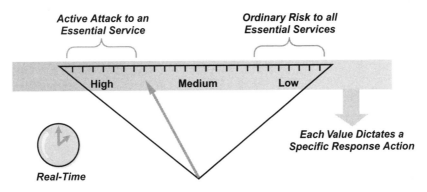

Figure 10.2 Rough dashboard estimate of cyber security posture.

into one generic measure of its security posture. This measure should be able to provide a rough estimate of the broad, organizational security risk at a given time. It should then weigh the likelihood and potential consequences of serious attack against the normal, everyday level of risk that an organization lives with every day. Presumably, risk on a day-to-day basis should be lower than during a serious incident, so it stands to reason that a rough metric could capture this status, perhaps as a high, medium, and low risk characterization (see Figure 10.2).

Factoring in all elements of situational awareness and any related challenges should create an overview of an organization's current security risk.

Unfortunately, the public perception of categorizing high, medium, and low security risks is that it does not provide useful information. This is certainly true for such measures as the public threat metric, which was used previously by the U.S. Department of Homeland Security to characterize risk. The problem with this metric was that it dictated no concrete actions to be taken by citizens. If risk was characterized as low, citizens were

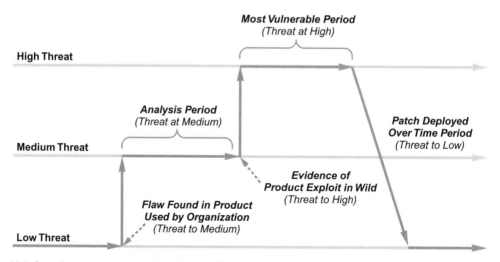

Figure 10.3 Security posture changes based on activity and response.

> Descriptors such as high, medium, and low to describe security risk are too vague to be helpful.

> Security risk levels should be set to correlate with actionable items.

warned to remain vigilant and on guard; if risk was characterized as medium or even high, the advice was essentially the same. Citizens were told to go on with their normal lives, but to be *somehow* more careful. Obviously, this type of advice causes confusion and is to be avoided in national infrastructure protection.

The only way a posture metric can be useful is if it is driven by real-time events and is connected directly to an explicit incident response program. When this is done, an ongoing rhythm develops where the situational status helps direct security management activity. This could involve some serious flaw being detected in an organization (which would drive the threat level upward), followed by detection of a real exploit in the wild (which would drive the threat level further upward), followed by a patch activity that fixes the problem (which would drive the threat level back down) (see Figure 10.3).

Regardless of public perception with respect to previous government threat metrics, any program of situational awareness for cyber security must include a broad characterization of real-time risk. The attributes of this broad characterization will be based on a much more detailed understanding of the real-time posture. Collectively, this posture is referred to as situational awareness and is based on an understanding of whether or not the infrastructure is under attack, which vulnerabilities are relevant to the local infrastructure, what sort of intelligence is available, the output of a risk management process, and information being generated by a real-time security operations center. These elements are described in the sections that follow.

Detecting Infrastructure Attacks

The process of determining whether an attack on national infrastructure is under way is much more difficult than it sounds. On the surface, one would expect that, by observing key indicators, making the determination that an attack has begun or is ongoing would seem straightforward. Correlating observed activity with profiles, signatures, and the like can provide a strong algorithmic basis, and products such as intrusion detection systems offer a means for implementation. These factors are misleading, however, and the truth is that no security task is more difficult and complex than the detection of an ongoing attack, especially if the adversary is skilled.

> There are many tools for detecting attacks, yet no single tool is comprehensive or foolproof.

To illustrate this challenge, suppose you notice that an important server is running in a somewhat sluggish manner, but you cannot diagnose the problem or explain why it is occurring. Obviously, this is suspicious and could be an indicator that your server has been attacked, but you cannot state this with any certainty. There could be a million reasons why a server is running slowly, and the vast majority of them have nothing to do with security. Suppose, however, that you discover a recently installed directory on the server that is filled with unfamiliar, strange-looking files. This will clearly raise your suspicion higher, but there are still numerous explanations that do not signal an attack. Perhaps, finally, someone in the enterprise steps forward and admits to running some sort of benign test on the server, thus explaining all of the errant conditions. The point is that confidence that a target is under attack will rise and fall, depending on the specifics of what is being observed. Obviously, there is a threshold at which the confidence level is sufficiently high in either direction to make a sound determination. In many practical cases, analysis never leads to such a confidence threshold, especially in complex national infrastructure environments (see Figure 10.4).

In our example, you eventually became confident that no attack was under way, but many scenarios are not terminated so cleanly. Instead, events expose a continuing stream of ongoing information that can have a positive, negative, or neutral effect on determining what is actually going on. In many cases, information that is incorrect or improperly interpreted has the effect of confusing the process. Relatively new technologies, such as mobile wireless services, tend to exhibit this property, especially in cases where a particular incident has never been seen before. The primary disadvantage of never determining the root cause of an attack is that the security posture cannot be accurately

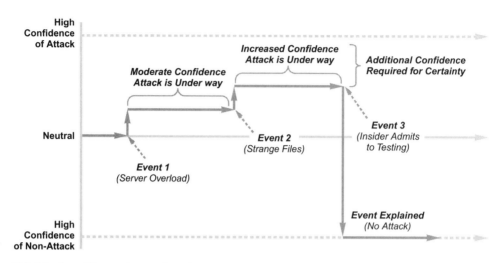

Figure 10.4 Attack confidence changes based on events.

> Determination of security risk level is a fluid process; it changes as new information is revealed or as situations change.

measured. This is especially troublesome when the attack is severe and targets essential national infrastructure services.

Managing Vulnerability Information

A common cynical view of computer security is that its experts are engaged in nothing more than a game of trivial pursuit around attack and vulnerability information. Support for this view is evident in the security books published to date, most of which contain page after page of esoteric attack specifics that are often long-since irrelevant. It is also evident in social circles at security and hacking conferences, where the discussion rarely addresses foundational topics of software engineering or system design but instead focuses on such trivia as which systems have which bugs in which versions on which hardware. Some security experts and hackers have become walking encyclopedias of such knowledge, even viewing information as the driver of power and skill. Anyone not possessing sufficiently detailed knowledge is thus tagged a newbie, lamer, or perhaps worse—a *manager*.

In spite of this odd phenomenon, situational awareness for national infrastructure protection does require a degree of attentiveness to daily trivia around vulnerability information. We refer to the information as trivia simply because, once addressed and fixed, the value of the information drops very close to zero. Nevertheless, it is important information to collect, and most national infrastructure teams use the default approach of *active opportunism*, where a set amount of effort is expended to gather as much data as possible and anything else that comes in is welcomed. The problem with active opportunism is that it will never be complete and cannot be depended upon for accurate management decisions. For example, the question of whether a given vulnerability has been coded into an exploit and made available on the Internet can be researched by one, two, or 50 people. If no evidence of such an exploit is found, then the weak conclusion can be drawn that it does not exist. Obviously, information about the vulnerability could be tucked away in some IRC discussion or on an obscure hacking site, but unless it is found or volunteered the security team will never know for sure.

The best one can hope for is to create as active and complete a vulnerability information-gathering process as possible. See the box for practical heuristics that have been useful for infrastructure protection in the past.

> Collecting daily trivia around vulnerability information should not be dismissed as unimportant but should be considered one of many methods of achieving situational awareness.

Practical Heuristics for Managing Vulnerability Information

- *Structured collection*—The root of all vulnerability management processes must be some sort of structured collection approach with means for assuring proper delivery of information, validating the source, cataloguing the information in a suitable taxonomy, and maintaining a useful database for real-time reference with provision for indexing and crawling vulnerability data in real-time. This structured approach should be integrated into all day-to-day cyber security activities so that accurate vulnerability information is available across the entire security infrastructure and team. Filters should exist to assure incoming data, as well as to ensure that external entities only obtain appropriate information (see Figure 10.5).
- *Worst case assumptions*—Many situations arise where a security team cannot determine whether some important piece of vulnerability-related information has actually been disclosed or has become known to an adversary group. The most mature and healthy approach in such scenarios is to assume the worst possible case. Most experts would agree that if the possibility arises that some vulnerability *might* be known externally, then it probably *is* known.
- *Nondefinitive conclusions*—Making definitive statements about national infrastructure security is not recommended. Too many cases exist where a security team draws the confident conclusion that a system is secure only to later obtain vulnerability-related information to the contrary. Experienced managers understand, for example, that they should always include caveats in security posture reports given to senior leaders in government or industry.
- *Connection to all sources*—Managing vulnerability information should include connections to all possible sources such as industry groups, vulnerability-reporting services, hacking conferences, internal employee reports, and customer data. Sometimes the most critical piece of vulnerability information comes from the most unlikely source.

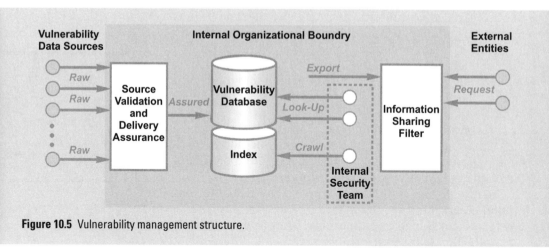

Figure 10.5 Vulnerability management structure.

Following the heuristics listed in the box above will help to ensure that the best available data is collected, stored, and used, but these heuristics can never provide assurance that the vulnerability management process is perfect. Instead, managers are strongly advised to follow three basic rules: (1) always assume that the adversary knows as much or *more* about your infrastructure than you do, (2) assume that the adversary is always keeping vulnerability-related secrets from you, and (3) never assume that you know everything relevant to the security of your infrastructure. Such complete knowledge is unattainable in large, complex national infrastructure settings.

Cyber Security Intelligence Reports

A technique commonly used in government intelligence community environments, but almost never in most enterprise settings, involves the creation and use of a regularly published (usually daily) intelligence report. For cyber security, such a report generally includes security-related metrics, indicators, attack-related information, root-cause analysis, and so on for a designated period. It is typically provided to senior management, as well as all decision-makers on the security and infrastructure teams. The report should also be indexed for searches on current and previous information, although this is not a common practice.

Although the frequency and content of intelligence reports should be tailored to the needs of the local environment, some

> Daily cyber security intelligence reports that are standard in government agencies would be equally useful in enterprise settings.

types of information that one would expect in any daily intelligence report include the following:

- *Current security posture*—The situational status of the current security risk would be required in any intelligence report, especially one issued over a daily or weekly interval (monthly intervals create too long a gap for information to be considered "intelligence").
- *Top and new security risks*—Characterization of the top risks, as well as any new risks, is also important to include in an intelligence report. Visualization and other techniques are often helpful to highlight changes in risk posture.
- *Automated metrics*—Security systems that generate metrics should provide input to the intelligence report, but care must be taken to avoid the creation of a voluminous document that no one will read. Also, raw output from some devices is indiscernible and should be either summarized or avoided in the report.
- *Human interpretation*—Ultimately, the most useful cyber security intelligence includes analysis by experienced and expert human beings who can interpret available security data and recommend suitable action plans. It is unlikely that this interpretation function will be automated in the near future.

> Human interpretation is bound to catch vulnerabilities that automated algorithms will miss.

The activity associated with the realization of a cyber security intelligence report can be viewed as an ongoing and iterative process made up of three tasks (see box).

Tasks for Creating a Cyber Security Intelligence Report

1. The first task involves *intelligence gathering* of available vulnerability and security posture data. This can be automated but should allow for manual submission from people who might have useful information to share. Many organizations do this gathering in the early morning hours, before the bulk of the business activity begins (a luxury that does not exist for global companies).

2. The second task involves *interpretation* and *publication* of the gathered data, not unlike similar processes in daily news publications. The interpretation should focus on the audience, never assuming too much or too little knowledge on the part of the reader. It is during this task that the human interpretive summary of the collected data is written.

3. The third task involves protected *dissemination* and *archiving* of the report for use by end users with a need to know. Report transmission is generally protected by encryption, and report archives and storage are protected by access controls (see Figure 10.6).

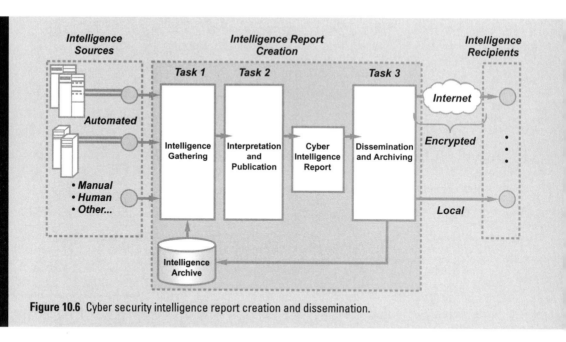

Figure 10.6 Cyber security intelligence report creation and dissemination.

One byproduct of creating an intelligence report is that it helps guide the local culture toward greater attentiveness to real-time security considerations. Everyone knows that, during an incident, response activity summaries will find their way to senior managers which tends to heighten concentration on the accuracy and completeness of the report. In addition, when an incident occurs that does not find its way into the report, managers can justifiably question the completeness of reporting around the incident.

Risk Management Process

Managers of essential national services must understand the security risks associated with their underlying infrastructure. Although this can be done using all sorts of fancy risk taxonomies, tools, and methodologies, the recommended approach is to simply maintain a prioritized list. Depending on the severity of the risks in the list, managers can decide to focus on a subset of the top ones, perhaps the top 10 or 20. Funding and resource allocation decisions for cyber security can then be driven by the security risk profile of the organization, keeping in mind that the list of risks will change with any adjustments in threat environment, technology deployment, or reported vulnerabilities.

Security risks must be tracked (listed) and prioritized to drive appropriate funding and resource allocation.

The generally agreed-upon approach to measuring the security risk associated with a specific component begins with two estimations:

- *Likelihood*—This is an estimate of the chances an attack might be successfully carried out against the specific component of interest.
- *Consequences*—This is an estimate of how serious the result might be if an attack were carried out successfully.

These two estimates must be performed in the context of an agreed-upon numeric range. The actual values in the range matter less than the relative values as the estimates increase and decrease. The simplest and most common values used are 1, 2, and 3, corresponding to low, medium, and high for both estimates. Once the likelihood and consequences have been estimated, risk is obtained by multiplying the values. Thus, if some component has a high likelihood of attack (value 3) and medium consequences resulting from an attack (value 2), then the associated risk is 3 times 2, or 6. If security measures are put in place to reduce the likelihood of an attack to medium (value 2), then the risk is now 2 times 2, or 4. Again, the absolute value of risk is less important than the relative value based on security decisions that might be made.

> The actual numeric value of a security risk is less important than its overall relative risk.

A useful construct for analyzing security decisions in infrastructures compares relative security risk against the costs associated with the recommended action. The construct allows managers to consider decision paths that might increase, decrease, or leave unaffected the security risk, with the balancing consideration of increased, decreased, or unaffected associated costs (see Figure 10.7).

To interpret the choices in the decision path structure, start at the middle of the diagram and consider the effects of each path labeled A through H. The path labeled G shows a security decision that increases costs in order to reduce risk. This is a normal management decision that is generally considered defensible as long as sufficient budget is available. Similarly, the path labeled C is also normal, as it accepts increased risk in order to reduce costs, which is unfortunately a common enough decision.

Interestingly, any decision path in the area shaded on the figure will be generally acceptable in most cases because the relationship between cost and risk is reasonable. The decision paths in the unshaded portion of the graph, however, are generally considered unacceptable because of the odd balance between the two factors. Decision path H, for example, increases costs with no impact on security risk. This case corresponds to the situation encountered all too often where a security safeguard is put in place that actually has zero impact on the risk profile.

> Increasing risks likely incur increased costs; assessing relative risk will help determine the value of investing in risk reduction.

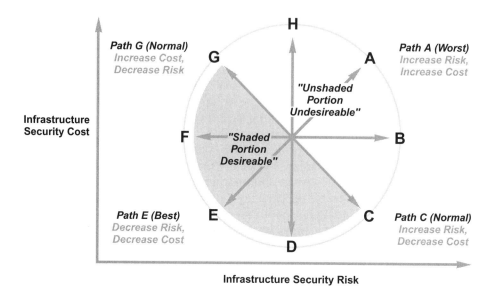

Figure 10.7 Risk versus cost decision path structure.

To summarize, all decisions about national infrastructure protection should be made in the context of two explicit management considerations: (1) maintaining a prioritized list of security risks to the system of interest, and (2) justifying all decisions as corresponding to paths in the shaded portion of the decision path structure shown in Figure 10.7. If these two simple considerations were mandatory, considerable time, effort, and money would be immediately saved for many infrastructure management teams.

Security Operations Centers

The most tangible and visible realization of real-time security situational awareness is the *security operations center* (SOC), also referred to as a *fusion center*. The most basic model of SOC operations involves multiple data, information, and intelligence inputs being fed into a repository used by human analysts for the purpose of operations such as interpretation, correlation, display, storage, archival, and decision-making. The SOC repository is constructed by active solicitation or passive acceptance of input information, and information processing combines human analysis with automated processing and visual display (see Figure 10.8).

Most SOC designs begin with a traditional centralized model where the *facility* is tied closely to the operations of the center.

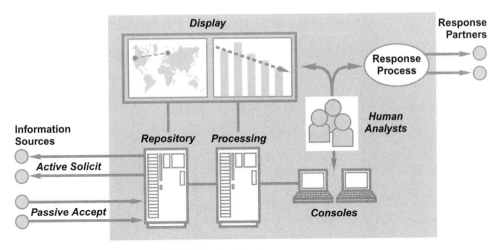

Figure 10.8 Security operations center (SOC) high-level design.

That is, methods and procedures are created that presume SOC resources, including all personnel, are located in one place with no need for remote coordination. All data is stored in a local repository that can be physically protected in one location. This approach has its advantages, because it removes so many coordination-related variables from the management equation. That said, an SOC can be created from distributed resources in geographically dispersed locations. Repositories can be distributed, and analysis can be performed using remote coordination tools. Generally speaking, this approach requires more work, but the main benefit is that more expert analysts can be recruited to such an approach, especially if the requirement is that 24/7 operations be supported. Experts can be hired across the globe in a "follow-the-sun" support arrangement.

> The advantage to global dispersal of SOC resources is an around-the-clock real-time analysis of security threats.

Typical operational functions supported in an SOC include all human interpretation of data by experts, management of specific incidents as they arise, support for 24/7 contact services in case individuals have security-relevant information to share, and processing of any alarms or tickets connected to a threat management or intrusion detection system. The 24/7 aspect of SOC operation is particularly useful to national-level situational awareness, because key infrastructure protection managers will know that they can obtain a security posture status at any time from a human being on call in the SOC. Government procurement efforts for national services should include requirements for this type of coverage in the SOC.

National Awareness Program

The goal of supporting a national-level view of security posture should not be controversial to most security and infrastructure managers. Everyone will agree that such a view is necessary and useful for supporting national infrastructure protection-related management decisions. The challenge, however, lies with the following important practical considerations:

- *Commercial versus government information*—To achieve full situational awareness at the national level will require considerable support from both commercial and government entities. Groups supplying security status information must be provided with incentives and motivations for such action. Patriotic justification helps, but global companies must be more deliberate in their sharing of information with any government.

- *Information classification*—When information becomes classified, obviously the associated handling requirements will increase. This can cause problems for data fusion. In fact, the essence of data compartmentalization for classified information is to prevent and avoid any type of fusion, especially with unclassified data. The result is that situational awareness at the national level will probably include two views: one unclassified and public, the other based on more sensitive views of classified information.

- *Agency politics*—Government agencies are famous for using *information* as a basis for political agendas, including support for project funding, hiring plans, and facility expansion. This tendency is counter to the goal of information sharing for situation awareness and must therefore be managed carefully.

- *SOC responsibility*—If a national SOC is to be realized, then some organization must be designated to run it. The decision as to whether this should be a defense- or civilian-related initiative is beyond the scope of this book, but most security experts agree that current defense-related awareness initiatives provide many of the elements required in a fully functioning SOC.

If these challenges are not addressed properly, the risk is that inaccurate views of situational awareness could arise. If an agency, for example, finds out about a vulnerability but decides to *not* share this information, then a hole emerges in any national-level risk estimation. Similarly, if a commercial organization is unable to receive and process classified information, then their view of current security risk posture will not be accurate. Attentiveness to managing these issues on a case-by-case basis, perhaps as part of a national SOC, would seem the best approach.

RESPONSE

Incident response is a vital part of any successful IT program and is frequently overlooked until a major security emergency has occurred, resulting in untold amounts of unnecessary time and money spent, not to mention the stress associated with responding to a crisis.

Kenneth van Wyk and Richard Forno[1]

The most familiar component of any cyber security program is the *incident response* process. This process includes all security-related activities that are initiated as a result of an attack that is imminent, suspected, under way, or completed. Incident response will generally be optimized to the local environment in an organization, but in most cases it will include at least the following four distinct process phases:

1. *Incident trigger*—Some warning or event must trigger the incident response process to be initiated. Obviously, if the trigger involves a system that has already been maliciously attacked, then the response must be focused on reconstitution and disaster recovery. If the trigger involves an early warning, then it is possible that the incident response process could avoid visibly negative effects.

2. *Expert gathering*—This involves a gathering together of the appropriate experts to analyze the situation and make recommendations. Most organizations have a base set of incident response staff that work all incidents and manage a repository of information related to all previous incidents. In addition, each incident will dictate that certain subject matter experts be brought into the process to work the details. These experts will also provide a local information base relevant to the incident at hand.

3. *Incident analysis*—Analysis of the incident is the primary task for the experts gathered during incident response. This can include detailed technical forensics, network data analysis,

[1]K. van Wyk and R. Forno, *Incident Response*, O'Reilly Media, Sebastopol, CA, 2001.

Cyber Attacks. DOI: 10.1016/B978-0-12-384917-5.00011-1

and even business process examination. Generally, the most difficult part of any analysis involves figuring out the underlying cause of the incident. Once this has been determined, developing the best solution is the key goal.

4. *Response activities*—The output of any incident response process will be a set of management recommendations on how to deal with the incident. These often include rebuilding systems, working around problems, informing customers, and the like. Providing this information to the correct individuals and organizations requires that the incident response teams be properly plugged into the specifics of which groups are responsible for which relevant functions.

Specific incident response processes will vary from organization to organization, but virtually every company and agency process is based on some version of these four elements and includes incident response processes local to an organization or that might exist as a special response resource for citizens, businesses, or government groups (see Figure 11.1)

In spite of the commonality inherent in the incident response processes found in various companies and agencies, great differences exist in their respective success patterns. The biggest differences reside in the relative effectiveness of incident response

> Most organizations have some form of incident response process in place that generally incorporates the same elements.

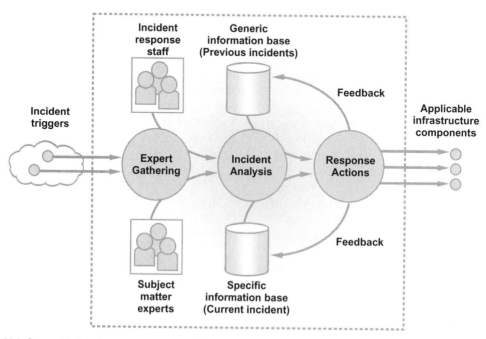

Figure 11.1 General incident response process schema.

in avoiding, rather than simply responding to, serious infrastructure problems. To optimize the early-warning aspect of incident response, certain key considerations must be well understood. These include a focus on pre- versus post-attack responses, detailed understanding of what constitutes a valid indication or warning, proper construction of how an incident response team should be managed, best practices in forensic analysis, optimal interactions with law enforcement, and good processes for recovering from disasters. These elements are explained in more detail below, with an emphasis on how national infrastructure response processes must be constructed and operated.

> Effective incident response is critical, but avoiding infrastructure problems in the first place will reduce the work required of the incident response team.

Pre- Versus Post-Attack Response

The most critical differentiating factor between incident response processes involves the two fundamental types of triggers that initiate response. The first type involves tangible, visible effects of a malicious attack or incident. These effects are usually noticed by end users in the form of slow application performance, clogged gateway performance, inability to get e-mail, slow or unavailable Internet access, and so on. Incident response in this case is usually urgent and is affected by the often vocal complaints of the user base. The second type of trigger involves early warning and indications information, usually embedded in some system or network management information. These triggers are usually not visible to end users but are prone to high levels of false positive responses, where the warning really does not connect to a malicious action.

> Early warning triggers are generally not visible to end users and are prone to high levels of false positives.

Incident response processes can thus be categorized into two specific approaches, based on the degree to which these triggers are addressed:

- *Front-loaded prevention*—This includes incident response processes that are designed specifically to collect indications and warning information for the purpose of early prevention of security attacks. The advantage is that some attacks might be thwarted by the early focus, but the disadvantage is that the high rate of false positive responses can raise the costs of incident response dramatically.
- *Back-loaded recovery*—This includes incident response processes that are designed to collect information from various sources that can supply tangible, visible information about attacks that might be under way or completed. This approach reduces the false positive rates but is not effective in stopping attacks based on early warning data.

> Combining front-loaded prevention with back-loaded recovery creates a comprehensive response picture; however, an emphasis on front-loaded prevention may be worth the increased cost.

Hybrid incident response processes that attempt to do both front-end and back-end processing of available information are certainly possible, but the real decision point is whether to invest the time, resources, and money necessary for front-loaded prevention. These two types of processes can be illustrated on the time line of information that becomes available to the security team as an attack proceeds. For front-loaded prevention, the associated response costs and false positive rates are high, but the associated risk of missing information that could signal an attack is lower; for a back-loaded response, these respective values are the opposite (see Figure 11.2).

> It is worth suffering through a higher number of false positives to ensure protection of essential national assets.

Back-loaded incident response might be acceptable for smaller, less-critical infrastructure components, but for the protection of essential national services from cyber attack the only reasonable option is to focus on front-end prevention of problems. By definition, national infrastructure supports *essential* services; hence, any process that is designed specifically to degrade these services misses their essential nature. The first implication is that costs associated with incident response for national infrastructure prevention will tend to be higher than for typical enterprise situations. The second implication is that the familiar false positive metric, found so often in enterprise settings as a cost-cutting measure, must be removed from the vocabulary of national infrastructure protection managers.

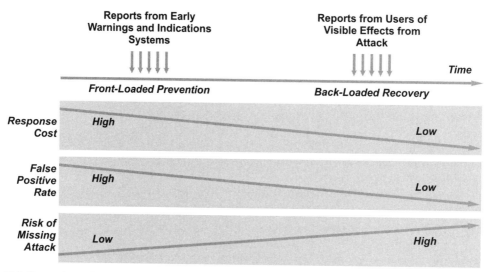

Figure 11.2 Comparison of front-loaded and back-loaded response processes.

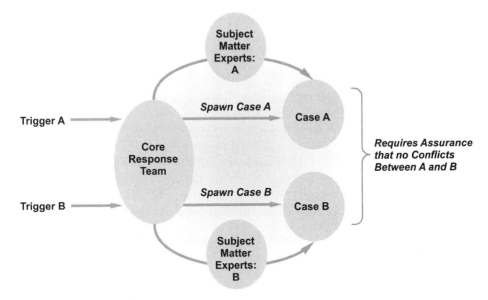

Figure 11.4 Management of simultaneous response cases.

In complex settings, the core incident response team is likely to be working multiple incidents simultaneously, generally with different sets of subject matter experts. Thus, response triggers will spawn new cases, which are worked in parallel to successful completion. In smaller environments, it is rare for multiple cases to be ongoing, but for larger, more complex critical infrastructure it is unusual to find times when multiple incident response cases are not being worked simultaneously. This leads to the unique incident response obligation for national infrastructure protection of ensuring that concurrent response activities do not mutually conflict (see Figure 11.4).

> Individuals on incident response teams need to ensure they are not working at cross-purposes with their colleagues.

The notion of managing simultaneous response cases is largely unexplored in conventional computer security. This is unfortunate, because every large organization eventually comes to the realization that this is not only possible but is generally the norm. Furthermore, those national attack scenarios with the most serious potential consequences to infrastructure routinely include multiple concurrent attacks aimed at the same company or agency. Response teams in a national setting must therefore plan for the possibility of multiple, simultaneous management of different incident response cases. Some considerations that help plan properly for this possibly include the following:

> It is unlikely that a large organization would not have simultaneous attack scenarios to face.

- *Avoidance of a single point of contact individual*—If a single individual holds the job of managing incident response processes, then the risk of case management overload emerges.

This might seem like a minor management detail, but given the importance of response, especially in a recovery scenario, avoidance of such weaknesses is a requirement.

- *Case management automation*—The use of automation to manage, log, and archive incident response cases will improve the productivity of the core incident response team and can lead to streamlined analysis, especially if previous case information is available for online, automated query and search.
- *Organizational support for expert involvement*—The entire organization must readily agree to provide experts for incident response when requested. This is not controversial when the process follows a back-loaded recovery method, because everyone is visually aware of the consequences of the incident. It is more challenging, however, when a front-loaded prevention approach is used and the triggers that initiate incident response are more subtle.
- *24/7 operational support*—Without full 24/7 coverage every day of every year, the success likelihood of managing multiple, concurrent incident response cases drops considerably. Most organizations integrate their incident response function into an SOC to ensure proper management coverage.

An interesting recent trend in infrastructure management involves the outsourcing of certain security operations to a third party. For status monitoring of security devices such as firewalls and intrusion detection systems, this is a reasonably mature activity and will have no materially negative effect on local security protection efforts (unless the outsourcing firm is incompetent). Even for certain SOC operations, outsourcing is often an excellent idea, especially because collection and correlation are always more effective if the vantage point is large. Outsourced SOC operations can also provide the security team with access to technical skills that may not reside locally.

Incident response processes, however, can easily become awkward for full outsourcing because of the embedded nature of prevention and recovery efforts for local infrastructure. Certainly, an outsourcing provider or vendor can and should be of assistance, and third-party SOC experts might offer excellent guidance and advice. Ultimately, however, incident response must be a local management function, and the organization will have no choice but to expend time, energy, and resources to ensure that the correct local management decisions are made. Third parties can never prioritize actions or tailor recovery procedures to the local environment as well as the organization itself. Instead, they should be used to augment local functions, to provide expert guidance, to automate processes, to manage equipment

| Outsourcing some aspects of security operations may make good business sense. |

| Companies cannot avoid complete responsibility for incident response by outsourcing the entire process; prioritizing and tailoring recovery procedures must be done locally. |

and networks, to support data collection and correlation, and to assist in recovery.

Forensic Analysis

Forensic analysis involves those activities required to investigate, at both a high level and a detailed lower level, the root cause and underpinnings of some event. Typical questions addressed during the forensic analysis process include:

- *Root cause*—How specifically was the target system attacked?
- *Exploits*—What vulnerabilities or exploits were used in the attack?
- *State*—Is the system still under an active state of attack by an adversary?
- *Consequences*—What components of the system were read, stolen, changed, or blocked?
- *Action*—What actions will stop this attack (if ongoing) or prevent one in the future?

To answer these difficult questions during incident response, forensic analysis requires the ability to drive deeply into a target system of interest, gathering relevant information but doing so in a manner than never destroys, affects, or changes key evidence. This is a critical requirement, because clumsy forensic analysis might overwrite important files, change important stamped dates on system resources, or overwrite portions of memory that include critical evidence. Forensic analysis is a difficult activity requiring great skill and competency, as well as the ability to investigate a system both manually and with the assistance of special tools (see Figure 11.5).

> Great care must be taken during forensic analysis not to change or destroy files or other critical evidence.

The forensic process is performed on a computer to determine how, when, and where some event on that computer might have occurred as the result of hardware, software, human, or network action. Corporate security groups, for example, often perform forensic analysis on a computer when the owner is suspected of violating some guideline or requirement. Law enforcement groups perform similar actions on computers seized from suspected criminals. Forensics can, however, be performed on a target much broader than a computer. Specifically, for the protection of essential national services, the organization must have the ability to perform forensic analysis on the entire supporting infrastructure.

> Forensic analysis can be specific (one computer) or broad based (entire supporting infrastructure).

The individual technical skills required to perform such broad forensic analysis are easy to write down, but qualified personnel are not always so easy to recruit and hire. This problem is so

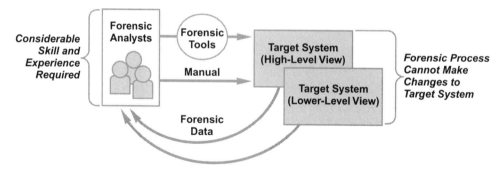

Figure 11.5 Generic high-level forensic process schema.

severe for most large organizations that it is not uncommon for a company or agency to have no local expert with sufficient skills to properly lead the investigation of a widespread infrastructure attack. This is unacceptable, because the only options for that organization are to locate such talent externally, and this will result in a less intimate evaluation process. Long-term employees who are committed to a career in an organization will always be more knowledgeable than consultants or third parties; furthermore, they will be suitably trusted to investigate an incident into the deep recesses of the local environment.

> An internal expert will be the one most likely to properly lead a company investigation, but few company employees have the requisite skills.

As such, the irony of forensic analysis is that most businesses and agencies would be wise to begin building and nurturing a base of talent with these skills. Typically, to maintain and satisfy forensic experts requires several things:

- *Culture of relative freedom*—Most good forensic analysts are creative individuals who learned their craft by exploring. They tend to maintain their skills by continuing to explore, so organizations must give them the freedom to seek and analyze systems, networks, applications, and other elements of interest. When they are working an incident, the target is obvious, but when they are not then managers must offer them the freedom to explore as they see fit. This is not easy for some managers, especially in relatively mature organizations with (ahem) long legacies of tight employee controls.
- *Access to interesting technology*—A related aspect of the local environment required to keep forensic analysts happy is constant access to interesting, changing, and emerging technology. What this means is that assigning your best forensic analysts to day-to-day operations around a single technology might not be the best idea.
- *Ability to interact externally*—Forensic analysts will also need the freedom to interact with their peer community and to

learn from experts outside the organization. This must be permitted and encouraged.

These environmental elements are not unique to forensic experts, but of all the skill sets required in a national infrastructure protection setting forensic analysis is the one that is the most difficult for an organization to obtain. Good forensic analysts can command the highest premium on the market and are thus difficult to keep, especially in a relatively low-paying government job. As such, attention to these quality-of-work-life attributes becomes more than just a good idea; instead, it becomes a requirement if the organization chooses to have the ability to perform forensic analysis as part of the overall incident response process.

> Investing in a good forensic analyst will be expensive but worthwhile for the protection of national security assets.

Law Enforcement Issues

A common issue faced by response teams is whether a given incident should be turned over to law enforcement for support. Most countries have laws that obligate response teams to contact law enforcement groups in the event of certain crimes; incident response teams must be familiar with these laws and must obey them without question. They must, in fact, be burned into incident response processes with full review by legal council in the organization. The issue of law enforcement involvement is also driven, however, by emotional considerations, especially when great time and effort have been directed toward dealing with some incident. The team often wishes to see tangible retribution, perhaps involving the bad guys actually going to jail.

> Carefully review local, regional, and national laws regarding when law enforcement must be contacted during a security incident.

In the end, however, interaction with law enforcement for infrastructure protection should follow a more deliberate and routine process. National infrastructure protection has a singular goal—namely, to ensure the continued and accurate delivery of essential services to the citizenry and businesses of a nation. This does not include the goal of catching bad guys and throwing them in jail, as much as security teams might like this result. The result is that discretionary law enforcement involvement should only be considered when the local security team believes that such enforcement could help with a current incident, perhaps through offering some relevant data or hints, or could help prevent a future incident by putting away some group that appears to be a repeat offender. A decision process for law enforcement involvement emerges as shown in Figure 11.6.

This decision process does recognize and support the clear requirement that crimes must be reported, but the figure also

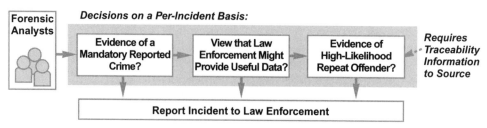

Figure 11.6 Decision process for law enforcement involvement in forensics.

Incident response teams should report relevant information to law enforcement, even if it does not result in arrest.

highlights a particularly fuzzy aspect of cyber security—namely, detecting suspicious behavior on a computer network usually does not constitute sufficient evidence of a crime being committed. Even if evidence of a break-in to a given system is observed, the argument could be made that no crime has occurred, especially if the break-in is the result of some automated process as one finds in a botnet attack.

The result is that national infrastructure protection teams will need to understand the decision process for law enforcement and follow it carefully during every incident. They will also need to create a local process for determining whether a crime has been committed in the context of their infrastructure. The result not only will optimize the interface between an organization and law enforcement but will also minimize the inevitable resource demands that will arise for the local team if law enforcement gets involved.

Disaster Recovery

The process of disaster recovery after a security attack is more mature than other aspects of incident response. This stems from the commonality that exists between recovery from attack and recovery from natural disasters such as floods, tornados, fires, and the like. Unfortunately, many large organizations charged with responsibility for national infrastructure do not properly address their obligation to include disaster recovery in their planning. Specifically, disaster recovery programs have three fundamental components, whether they are driven by concerns of malicious attack or natural disaster (see box).

Three Components of a Disaster Recovery Program

- *Preparation*—The decision to prepare in advance for disaster recovery is easy to make but much more difficult to support in practice. Operational funding is usually the stumbling block, because the process of preparing for disaster in advance involves more than just writing down a list of potential actions. Instead, it often requires architectural changes to avoid single points of potential failure. It could require installation of safe, redundant means for communication between recovery teams, and it could even require upgrades to cyber security systems to ensure proper protection through a disaster.

- *Planning*—An essential element in a disaster recovery program is an explicit plan that is written down and incorporated into all operational methods and procedures. The plan can be continually improved as the organization deals with real disasters. For example, many organizations who relied on the use of commercial airplanes to shuttle equipment to disaster sites found that this did not work well in the aftermath of 9/11.

- *Practice*—The decision to practice for disasters is also an expensive one, requiring that teams of experts be funded to support mock drills. The best way to practice for a disaster is to create a realistic scenario and work through the specifics of the written plan. Usually, this will involve the use of spare computing or networking capacity that is set aside in a hot configuration (see Figure 11.7).

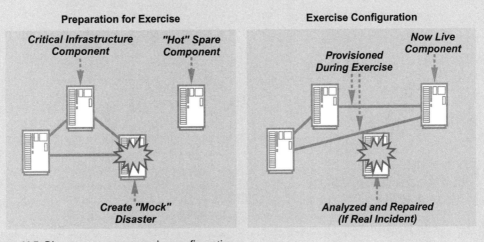

Figure 11.7 Disaster recovery exercise configurations.

Realistically, very few organizations actually practice for disasters. It requires a discipline that is generally missing from most enterprise system and network teams and can only work if the senior leadership team makes it a priority. Sadly, the only time disasters are considered is after they occur, especially after they have some impact on the local environment. This familiar process

> Proper planning for disaster response and recovery requires time and discipline, but the outcome is well worth the effort.

of taking disasters seriously only after they occur is something we have all witnessed in our society, especially as it relates to natural disasters and terrorism. For proper protection of national infrastructure from cyber attack, this attitude must be adjusted.

National Response Program

The most important function in any national response program involves emergency coordination among government, business, citizens, and other nations during a cyber attack incident. The respective interfaces must be identified and managed as part of response planning. National programs can provide centralized coordination, but intrasector coordination should also be encouraged (see Figure 11.8).

This coordination function would seem obvious, but most existing national emergency response programs and computer emergency response team (CERT) programs tend to focus on dissemination of vulnerability-related information. This is useful, especially for smaller organizations that have no security team, but this focus tends to leave a gap in national-level coordination should a major national incident occur. Amazingly, at the time of this writing, such a major national incident has yet to occur, but if one should happen soon then national coordination in the United States is unlikely to be smooth. This is unacceptable and requires immediate attention to properly protect national infrastructure from the effects of cyber attack.

Figure 11.8 National response program coordination interfaces.

SAMPLE NATIONAL INFRASTRUCTURE PROTECTION REQUIREMENTS

Any discussion of computer security necessarily starts with a statement of requirements.

U.S. Department of Defense "Orange Book" (*Trusted Computer System Evaluation Criteria***, DoD 5200.28-STD)**

Readers of this book associated with enterprise organizations should consider translating the security material presented in this book into an action plan relevant to their local environment. For the majority, this will involve creating a set of new security requirements for infrastructure protection. Valid scenarios might include public officials embedding new security requirements for collection or correlation into a Request for Proposal (RFP). They might also include enterprise security engineers writing new types of security policy requirements on the filtering of distributed denial of service attack (DDOS) aimed at their company, as well as researchers and product engineers embedding new security requirements for deceptive honey pots into their innovation plans.

Obviously, the best way for any requirement to properly match a target environment is for it to be tailored specifically to that environment. This requires that the security engineer writing the requirement must possess an understanding of local constraints, along with sufficient insight into the purpose and intent of the new security control. For this reason, it is not practical to propose in this appendix a set of requirements for national infrastructure protection that will perfectly address all cases. Instead, presented below is a set of *sample* base requirements that provide context and illustration for readers determined to embed some of the ideas presented in this book into their local program.

Each sample requirement is written as a constraint on how a given organization might operate. In fact, the terminology for our samples follows the general format: "*The organization must …*," and readers should be capable of tailoring the statement to a locally specific format: "… *do such and such under conditions XYZ in environments ABC for purposes IJK.*" The requirements are not comprehensive, so the idea of cutting and pasting the examples to create a new policy would be a bad idea. The requirements are also not complete, so one should not presume that the sample requirements on correlation, for example, provide a sufficient summary of the material presented on that topic. Instead, this appendix is offered as a pedagogical tool to help readers create requirements that not only may be effective at protecting infrastructure but are also meaningful and practical in local environments.

Sample Deception Requirements (Chapter 2)

In this section, we provide three sample deception requirements that will reduce the risk of attack to a given target infrastructure component by introducing uncertainty to the attacker and by creating a means for analyzing live attacks. Readers are warned, however, that locally relevant legal issues must be carefully attended to before deploying any sort of honey pot. Attorneys who are knowledgeable in the area of practical deception deployment are unfortunately quite scarce.

The organization must …

(DEC-1) … *operate deceptive honey pot functionality, in connection with infrastructure supporting essential services, that is attractive and locally accessible to malicious insiders.* This requirement ensures that effort has been made to operate trap functionality focused on catching insiders, including employees, consultants, visitors, and contractors, who might demonstrate malicious intent to commit system sabotage or data exfiltration. The deployment does not have to be extensive but should be tailored to the size and scope of the infrastructure component being protected. The decision to run in stealth or non-stealth mode can be a local decision. Demonstration of compliance should include a test in which the honey pot is shown to be accessible from an internal network and is designed well enough to be reasonably convincing to a typical internal adversary.

(DEC-2) … *operate deceptive honey pot functionality in connection with supporting essential services that is attractive and externally accessible to malicious outsiders.* This requirement ensures that effort has been made to operate trap functionality that is focused on malicious outsiders who might target organizational resources via the Internet or some other external access point, such as an extranet or virtual private network (VPN). The deployment also does not have to be extensive but should be tailored to the target environment and can be done in a stealth or non-stealth manner, depending on local needs. Penetration testing from the Internet can be used to check compliance.

(DEC-3) ... *provide evidence that all deceptive honey pot functionality is associated with explicit management and support systems for the purpose of initiating response.* This requirement ensures that the organization has sufficient back-end systems for the deception to be effective, especially if it is done in stealth mode. This requirement is best met by a honey pot alarm notification system connected to human beings trained to interpret the results and direct a response action. Without such back-end support, the deception is unlikely to operate properly. It is also generally important that the back-end systems include means for dealing with innocent authorized users who gain access to a honey pot inadvertently.

Sample Separation Requirements (Chapter 3)

In this section, we introduce six sample requirements on how firewalls, access controls, and filters can be effectively used to help protect national infrastructure. The inclusion of filtering requirements for mobile wireless systems will be controversial in the vast majority of environments simply because such functionality might not be locally accessible or available through any practical means.

The organization must ...

(SEP-1) ... *proactively redirect or filter live DDOS traffic before it reaches local network ingress points.* This requirement ensures that the organization takes steps to reduce the risk associated with inbound DDOS attacks. A service provider operating filters on a large capacity backbone is a good option here. The amount of filtering should be expressed as a multiple of inbound ingress capacity. Obviously, this multiple must be greater than one—and the greater, the better. The filters must not operate on the ingress gateway, for obvious reasons (do the math). Testing of this capability should be done carefully, as the creation of a live, inbound attack can easily get out of hand. (Disaster recovery procedures should always be in place before creation of a live test attack on anything.)

(SEP-2) ... *provide evidence that inbound attacks on externally accessible applications cannot produce an amplification-based*

DDOS attack on local network egress points. This requirement ensures that the organization is addressing the risk of inbound amplification attacks on poorly designed, externally accessible applications. The evidence required here most likely will be the result of a set of functional tests, code reviews, and requirements audits. The idea is to check for evidence that small questions at an application cannot produce very large responses to the external requestor. In the most complex application environments, this effort will not remove the egress DDOS risk, but the evidence gathering process should identify obvious problems. It should also raise general awareness of the risk for developers creating new applications.

(SEP-3) … *flexibly enforce network access controls (firewalls) between designated groups of insiders, especially those working in direct support of essential services.* This requirement ensures that the organization is using internal firewalls to create trusted internal domains. Casual insiders, including the majority of a typical employee base, should not have the ability to view, change, or block a broad set of internal resources as a result of their special access as employees, contractors, or visitors. This is especially true for access to the systems supporting essential services. Certainly, employees working on a specific component might have the ability to cause local problems, but this effect should be limited to the local component. This can be accomplished with firewalls, access lists on routers and switches, encryption-based systems, and other types of security mechanisms. Penetration testing from Intranet locations can be used to establish compliance.

(SEP-4) … *flexibly enforce network access controls (firewalls) between organizational resources and any untrusted external network, including any mobile wireless infrastructure.* The familiar part of this requirement involves firewalls between an organization and external, untrusted networks such as the Internet. Almost every organization on the planet will be able to meet this requirement, albeit with a ragged perimeter model that might include hundreds or even thousands of access exceptions in their rule base. The unfamiliar part of the requirement is that mobility-based access over wireless carrier networks is included in the mediation. Because most companies and agencies do not have easy access to an enterprise mobile policy enforcement engine, cooperation with the mobile network carrier may be required (and don't be surprised if your carrier has some trouble supporting your needs, as this is very new territory).

(SEP-5) … *stop inbound e-mail and web-based viruses, spam, and other malware before they reach network ingress points* *to any local infrastructure supporting essential services.* This requirement ensures that unwanted inbound traffic is collected before it hits the ingress point to a target network—most likely the existing organizational Intranet. This greatly reduces the risk of a volume-based attack using these services and simplifies gateway security requirements. Efficiency and cost reduction concerns are a good byproduct in this approach, even though they are not the primary motivations for inclusion. Compliance can be established here through simple injection of inbound test traffic aimed at the target.

(SEP-6) … *demonstrate that separation controls based on organizational security policy are in place for cloud-hosted applications, resources, and systems in support of essential services.* This requirement ensures that the use of cloud infrastructure for applications, hosting, storage, and other components supporting essential services is properly protected based on organizational security policy rules. With increasing adoption of cloud services for software, storage, applications, and systems, this requirement is likely to gradually develop into a set of best practices for cloud-based security. Integration of existing organizational identity management functionality is likely to be one of the most challenging aspects of cloud security.

Sample Diversity Requirements (Chapter 4)

In this section, we introduce two diversity requirements that will not be easy to implement in most environments. The practical reality is that most chief information officers (CIOs) have intentionally created networks that are lacking diversity, standardized, and cost effective but that are also susceptible to failure by a single vendor and do not have sufficient backup by an alternate vendor. The desktop operating system is a good example. These requirements remain, nevertheless, powerful weapons for reducing the cascading effect of certain attacks and should thus be championed by the security team. The decision not to follow a diverse path should be made only after careful debate and consideration of all available options. A compromise might involve restricting the diversity to highly focused areas associated with especially critical systems.

The organization must …

(DIV-1) … *provide evidence that no single vendor failure or compromise can produce a cascading effect across any combination of application, computing, or network components supporting essential services.* This requirement reduces the risk that a cascading chain of failure can occur in critical infrastructure because of a common vendor thread in a technology. As suggested above, this is a tough requirement for most organizations to meet on the desktop, given the pervasiveness of a common architecture and set of applications. It is nevertheless critical that the cascading problem be addressed through attention to diversity. Compliance can be checked manually.

(DIV-2) … *utilize at least one live, alternative backup vendor in a substantive manner for all software, PCs, servers, and network components in support of essential services.* This requirement implies one possible component of meeting DIV-1 by dictating a live, alternative backup. The requirement might be tailored in practice to a target percentage; for example, the requirement might state that at least 10% of all organizational PC operating systems in support of essential services be provided by a backup vendor. Compliance can be checked manually here as well.

Sample Commonality Requirements (Chapter 5)

In this section, two commonality requirements are included that should be well suited for integration into most environments. The goal for most organizations will be to improve policy and compliance strategies rather than to create them from scratch.

The organization must …

(COM-1) … *have a written security policy, with training programs for decision-makers, auditable mechanisms for compliance, and written processes for punishing violators.* The familiar part of this requirement is that a security policy must be in place with mechanisms for compliance. The unfamiliar part involves training emphasis for decision-makers and written processes for dealing with violations.

(COM-2) … *demonstrate full organizational compliance to at least one recognized information security standard verified by an external auditor.* This requirement ensures that the organization has targeted at least one reasonably well-known and accepted security standard for compliance. While there are some differences between standards, the reality is that the recognized ones all include a basic core set of requirements that dictate essentially the same sort of controls. Thus, it really doesn't matter, in the vast majority of cases, which standard is selected as long as at least one is being used.

Sample Depth Requirements (Chapter 6)

In this section, three sample requirements are offered that are intended to improve the depth of security mechanism layers for essential services. The requirements focus on access, failure, integrity, and encryption; readers can easily extrapolate this emphasis to other technical or security areas.

The organization must ...

(DEP-1) ... *provide evidence that no individual, inside or outside the organization, can directly access systems supporting an essential service without at least two diverse security authentication challenges.* This requirement ensures that two types of authentication are used in accessing essential infrastructure. Local interpretation would be required to determine if the selected methods are sufficiently diverse. A personal identification number (PIN) with a handheld authenticator, for example, is often touted as providing sufficient two-factor validation of identity; however, a group might locally interpret these two factors as a single challenge.

(DEP-2) ... *provide evidence that failure of any one protection system cannot lead to a direct compromise in any application, computing, or networking functionality supporting essential services.* This requirement ensures that failure of a single protection system cannot compromise the overall mission. This might be achieved via network-based security, duplication and distribution, or some other means. Firewalls, in particular, are often single points of defense that require a corresponding alternative protection method.

(DEP-3) ... *provide evidence that all information, whose unauthorized disclosure could directly affect the integrity and operation of any essential service, is subjected to at least two diverse levels of encryption during both storage and transmission.* This requirement ensures that the most critical information for essential services be encrypted twice using diverse means. The interpretation of what constitutes "most critical information" can be negotiated locally and should truly correspond to only that information whose confidentiality is critical to the operation of an essential service. Thus, one could imagine this being a very small portion of information in limited types of circumstances. End-to-end plus link-level encryption is an example of how this requirement might be met in some cases.

Sample Discretion Requirements (Chapter 7)

This section introduces two sample requirements on how information is handled. The requirements are reasonably conventional, and many organizations will find that complying with these examples is not challenging. The real goal, however, is to create a culture of discretion in an organization; unfortunately, it is not a trivial exercise to write objective requirements that measure how well a culture is suited to critical infrastructure protection. The sample requirements below at least provide a start.

The organization must …

(DIS-1) *… provide evidence that organizational information related to any essential service is properly marked and that such markings are suitably enforced.* This requirement should include evidence, perhaps through an unplanned audit, that all documents contain the proper markings. So many organizations violate this simple principle, and this is a shame, because it provides powerful protection against certain types of data leakage. Data leakage tools, for example, can be tuned to detect properly marked documents that might be inadvertently transmitted to an untrusted destination.

(DIS-2) *… provide evidence that organizational staff associated with essential services is fully trained in local policies for how information is handled and shared externally.* Compliance analysis here might require some interpretation, as most organizations will have some level of training. The key question is whether this training is considered acceptable, as well as how well the organization ensures that all staff completes the training on a regular basis. Obviously, if any of the requirements described here are inserted in the organizational policy, then training must be updated accordingly.

Sample Collection Requirements (Chapter 8)

This section introduces two sample collection requirements that help establish more formal, written policies on how information is collected for security purposes. A key goal in establishing any type of collection policy is to ensure that basic privacy considerations are fully attended to, in a manner that allows the security team sufficient access to data to identify early indicators and to perform proper security forensic analysis.

The organization must …

(COL-1) *… provide evidence that a set of criteria has been established for which types of information in which contexts* *should be collected and stored by the organization.* The criteria for collection and storage must certainly include attention to various factors, including privacy, but the focus here is on security. The intent is to require that a set of criteria is in place for what is collected and stored, with the goal of ensuring that relevant attacks and indicators will be detectable in the collected data. If the collection process involves loose sampling of packets on a small percentage of network links, for example, then the likelihood of detecting an important security indicator might be low.

(COL-2) *... provide evidence that collection systems are in place to gather in real time and store in a secure manner all desired information from applications, systems, and networks.* Having real-time access to data enables early warnings of attack. If the collection process is done in a casual batch mode, perhaps employing daily, weekly, or even monthly reports, then great damage could occur to an essential service before a corresponding trend might even be noted.

Sample Correlation Requirements (Chapter 9)

This section introduces two sample correlation requirements that help focus an organization on a structured approach to ensuring that proper data analysis is being performed in an environment that allows for awareness and response.

The organization must ...

(COR-1) *... provide evidence that effective algorithms are in place to correlate relevant information in real-time toward actionable results.* Correlation algorithms do not have to be complex; rather, they must be properly in place and effective in their operation, and they should lead to some sort of actionable security processes. In truth, complex algorithms might not even be desirable. I've seen simple packet counters provide more relevant information than complex pattern-matching signature-based intrusion prevention systems.

(COR-2) *... provide evidence that correlative output (presumably in a security operations center) is connected to organizational awareness and response functions.* This requirement ensures that the correlation, collection, awareness, and response functions are all connected. The presumption that this be done in a security operations center is based on the practical observation that most organizations that try to ensure such connections do so in a security operations center.

Sample Awareness Requirements (Chapter 10)

This section introduces three sample requirements that focus on embedding situational awareness capabilities into the day-to-day infrastructure of an organization. Particular emphasis is placed on real-time, comprehensive capabilities.

The organization must …

(AWA-1) *… provide evidence that cyber security intelligence information related to essential services is collected on a regular basis and disseminated to decision makers on a timely basis.* This requirement ensures that an intelligence collecting process is in place. It should include mechanisms for safely obtaining raw data, for interpreting the data in a way that protects its integrity as well as any privacy constraints, and for creating a set of actionable intelligence information for cyber security control.

(AWA-2) *… provide evidence that a real-time security operations function exists that coordinates any preventive or response actions based on collected information and correlative analysis (presumably in an operations center).* This requirement ensures that the organization has a means for taking action as a result of collected intelligence. Too many groups create fancy security intelligence collection processes, render interesting patterns on large glowing wallboards, and can provide anecdotes about all sorts of previous security attacks. It is far less common, however, to find an organization that truly coordinates action based on available information.

(AWA-3) *… provide evidence that a real-time and comprehensive threat and vulnerability management process is in place and that relevant data is used to minimize security risk to all equipment and software supporting essential services.* It is not uncommon to find a threat and vulnerability management process in place in an organization. Assurance is not always available, however, that the process is real-time or comprehensive. That is, the data might become available in an arbitrary manner, and coverage issues for all equipment and software supporting essential services might not be properly considered.

Sample Response Requirements (Chapter 11)

This section introduces two sample requirements on how an organization performs incident response. The emphasis is on enhancing existing response processes to include more proactive responses to indicators as well as improved documentation and metrics.

The organization must ...

(RES-1) *... provide evidence that the organization has the ability to respond to indicators and warning signals in advance of an attack on any critical resource.* This requirement ensures that an incident response can be initiated based on indicators, rather than just outages. Every organization has the ability to notice that things have gone completely haywire (e.g., network down, e-mail not working), but only more aggressive groups have built processes for responding to more subtle data, perhaps from network devices, servers, or security systems.

(RES-2) *... provide evidence that the organization maintains documentation and metrics on the root cause of past security problems, as well as the effectiveness of response activities for past and present security incidents.* Amazingly, few solicitations include this requirement; in fact, as a member of a service provider security team for the past 25 years, I've only seen this partially required a couple of times in major government procurements. More generic past practice requirements are often specified by government buyers (rarely, if ever, in commercial settings), but the specifics regarding root cause metrics, documented effectiveness, and other statistics are rarely dictated.

INDEX